Dedicated to the Truth!

Table of Contents

A Personal Thought ix
Introduction xi

1. Leviathan : The Sea-Dragon 1
   Creation 2
   The Initiation of Creation 3
   Leviathan 4
   Join the Cause : A Rebellion Attempt 4
   War and Judgment 6
   Cell Block Ice 8
   Thawed: Freedom from Restraints 9

2. GOD'S Declaration For Leviathan 13
   An Interpretation of Job 16

3. Leviathan's Realm 21
   Go West 22
   Too Big To Fail 26
   LOOK 35
   The Next Generation 46

4. Leviathan's Power 55
   Arrogance: A Reasoning Behind Disaster 55
   Which Way Will I Go ? 60
   Believe Us... And The Movement 67
   Allurement 73

5. Other Names and Faces of Leviathan 81
   An Entity of the Sea 83
   His and Hers 86
   Fish Food 88

Reflective Names: The King of Children ...... .90
   Reflective Names and Characteristic
   References. 91
   Defeated 92

6. **A Defeated Foe**. 95
   A One-Two Punch 95
   A Date with Defeat 96
   Surviving the Movement. 98
   Reeling in Another Catch at Sea. 103
   How Humanity Can Defeat Leviathan. 108
   Sample Prayer. 112
   Parting Words. 114

A Personal Thought

To some, at times there may be certain topics in this publication which may appear a little mystical, magical, or even unbelievable. Having received divine revelation and understanding from the Spirit of GOD, along with decades of experience and research, I have found the information contained within these pages to be true.

By the will of Father GOD through Christ-Jesus, all the enclosed information has been gathered together. This information was gathered in order to expose and reveal many wonderous things to mankind.

May the obtainable knowledge and insight within this publication be an empowerment for your journey through life. And may these words in this book be used to further your GOD-given destiny.

Introduction

Numerous tales have been told around the world. Some tales speak of mysterious creatures that have secretly lurked in the oceans, rivers, and lakes on our planet. Most of these stories regarding watery entities have transcended from diverse cultures and varied in their descriptions concerning the many different water-dwellers.

Granted, some of those accounts of an encounter with water beings have been fabricated or made up. Other stories were perhaps told for pure entertainment. After all, many people enjoy a good fishing story or two. But every reported sighting and encounter with those from down below should not be disregarded just because some reports were falsified.

To speak to any notion of exaggerated tales, it must be made clear that fake fishing tales will not be the focus of any portion of this book. One purpose for these writings is to aid humanity in a practical awareness, while revealing the truth concerning a supernatural being from the seas named Leviathan.

Before turning the pages to begin such a voyage into mystical and empowering knowledge, two simple requests are asked. First, please keep an open mind concerning the information presented. Second, allow GOD to show you exactly what HE would have you know regarding Leviathan.

Chapter 1

Leviathan:
The Sea-Dragon

THE TERM LEVIATHAN is commonly used in many languages around the world. This phrase can represent some simplistic implications. For example, if someone was to examine the meaning of "Leviathan" in most dictionaries, similar explanations would be given as to that particular word's definition. Collectively, a general description of how most people have come to initially describe a Leviathan can be broke down into two ideas:

1. A large sea animal
2. Something large in form

The terminology of a Leviathan, as given through these customary understandings, is a correct interpretation. A Leviathan can be classified as a sizeable sea animal or something large in form.

However, simple basic information to directly single out just any type of Leviathan is not this publication's primary goal. The objective is to reveal uncommonly known information and hidden details concerning the one for whom the term had been cast: Leviathan.

Just as a jostling current might occur at sea to initiate a flow forward, something may initially have had to surge in reverse. With that idea in mind let us venture back to the beginning of time before planet earth. Here at the initiation of creation is where a particular journey must commence.

Creation

There have been a variety of accounts, regarding creation, which have circulated throughout mankind over vast amounts of time. The version used in this book will come from the King James Version of *The Holy Bible*.

The Holy Bible is a book divided into both an Old and New Testament, collectively containing sixty-six mini-books within its writings. These mini-books were penned by many individuals from various eras. Although each book was physically written by human hands, each author received divine inspiration from GOD in what to write.

With regard to creation let's begin with *The Holy Bible's* first book in the Old Testament: Genesis. Genesis 1:1 presents a clear revelation as to what transpired in the beginning.

> "In the beginning God created the heaven and the earth."

It is plainly stated in the verse whom it was that brought everything into existence. *"God"* chose to create *"the heaven and the earth."*

However, to continue on in this documented story a turn of events occur in Genesis 1:2.

> "And the earth was without form, and void; and darkness was upon the face of the deep. And the Spirit of God moved upon the face of the waters."

Seemingly from the first sentence of this particular verse it appears as if something had taken place in the cosmos. Apparently *"God created"* everything in verse 1, yet verse 2 describes a completely opposite environment. The environment has become surprisingly a place *"without form, and void"* according to *Holy Scripture*.

With that information one may inquire what could have happened to explain such a transition and change? In order to elaborate on the events which led up to such an alteration and what occurred afterward, a story will be presented.

The Initiation of Creation

The ultimate and uncontainable I AM, commonly known to mankind as GOD, chose to begin bringing into existence form. The initiation of all creation (as we know it) would now be under way.

One of the first divine objectives was to create other energies and forces. As GOD willed, some of the first life forms were made to serve the Almighty. These newly created beings were called Archons, which mean "first ones."

Numerous Archons had been created for various jobs to aid in a massive construction project, with each one possessing unique talents and abilities gifted to them by their Creator. Other forms and powers were made with special capabilities and attributes also. So it did not matter whether you were an Archon, angel, or other, as long as you were a devoted servant to the Most High.

Leviathan

One certain Archon went by the name of Leviathan. This being was created with substantial might and power. Without failure and right from the beginning he always took his assigned task from GOD seriously.

Not long after Leviathan started to serve in the kingdom he began to acquire some recognition throughout the heavens. Many beheld this Archon openly demonstrate and exert his marvelous gifts and abilities in service to GOD. These attributes and efforts continued to position Leviathan into an ever-growing leadership role.

Abiding in a high knowledge and supernatural understanding through his Creator, the Archon attained and strived for an element of perfection. With no hesitation when placed with any assignment, Leviathan quickly proceeded to comply with his master's will. While he focused on accomplishing the will of GOD, another began to focus on him.

One particular angel became aware of Leviathan's movements. That individual started to observe many things the Archon did. This angelic being bore the name Lucifer.

Join the Cause: A Rebellion Attempt

Lucifer was conscious of Leviathan and his growing popularity with various celestial inhabitants. These insights appealed to Lucifer because he had some ideas of his own to take over portions of the cosmos. Thoughts emerged

Leviathan: The Sea-Dragon

that if he could hook Leviathan and control him, it might be possible to take command of all those who looked up to, admired, or respected the Archon.

Without delay the angel began to make it a priority to come into contact with Leviathan whenever possible. At first Lucifer carefully chose the words he spoke when they crossed paths, because he needed to know exactly where that Archon's loyalty lay. However, after many interactions with one another Lucifer eventually found out Leviathan held a hidden secret.

Externally the Archon acted very dedicated to the cause, but something was buried underneath the surface. Because of so many successful accomplishments he already achieved, Leviathan started to think of himself very highly. His thoughts may have even gotten to the point of vainglory.

Soon after he discovered Leviathan's weakness the rebel angel planned to make his move. Time became a factor because Lucifer was busy in building a revolt against GOD'S authority and striving with an attempt to be equal to the Almighty. And if his diabolical plan had any chance for success it needed everyone possible to participate, including Leviathan.

At first the Archon seemed to reject the slightest hint of insubordination, but surprisingly did not raise any alarm. Nonetheless, those thoughts of who could stand against the Creator kept continuously replaying in his mind.

On the other hand, the attempts for his conversion would not be over yet because Lucifer was not through.

Eventually convinced by various manipulations and bribes, the Archon finally of his own free will joined Lucifer's rebellion to go to war. It was a well-kept secret that

Leviathan did not agree to become involved just because he felt simply overwhelmed to please Lucifer. On the contrary, this Archon had many other reasons to join.

Part of the deal entailed Leviathan bringing Lucifer a vast number of supporters by whatever means. For that particular service Leviathan would be compensated a steep price, which included becoming one of three personal assistants to Lucifer himself. This position of power also carried with it the title of crown prince.

War and Judgment

Initially the growth of the secretive army met with some resistance because not everyone became delusional by the angel's words and those who spoke them. However, with the aid of many new forces from Leviathan's camp certain portions of the cosmos began to systematically fall deeper into Lucifer's grasp. By the time the last crown prince took the oath of office and was sworn in, their secret war had begun to take hold of areas throughout the universe.

With Lucifer and his aids succeeding without many interruptions, the focus of the war changed toward the invasion date of GOD'S celestial city. Many in the heavenly ranks had already been bribed, disillusioned, or enticed. These angelic beings already made their deals, received their promises, and took their oaths to Lucifer and the new kingdom. Almost one-third of GOD'S creation stood ready, willing and secretly pledging their loyalty to another.

The war for the heavens was at hand, as the atmosphere all around seemed to take on an eerie presence of what was coming. Lucifer's hidden forces quickly mustered and went on the move. No more need for concealment, for the time had come where it was too late for anyone to turn back. Now these rebellious actions were placed in motion and would simply have to follow through regardless of the consequences.

When the invading forces began their march into GOD'S holy city, a variety of clashes occurred simultaneously as angelic host confronted foreign invader. The violent shaking of these battles only continued to multiply and intensify. This war became so tremendous it escalated to a degree where the very heavens quaked from all the conflict.

At that very moment, less than a split second of time, GOD grew weary of this conflict. The Almighty spoke, and through GOD'S majestic will the war ceased. The war was over.

Without hesitation the heavenly host quickly brought under subjection the invading army, as these rebellious creatures trembled at the wroth voice of the great I AM. Trembling also was Lucifer and the once mighty Leviathan.

Certain severe judgments were ushered out instantaneously upon those who tried to overthrow GOD'S order, because a public example must be made for all to see. After those specific actions had been employed Lucifer and his defeated militia were taken from the Almighty's holy presence.

Bound, chained, crushed, and defeated, these celestial criminals were cast from heaven and thrust to an awaiting place of holding. The destination of their confinement would be a planet. This holding place was to be earth.

Interestingly enough, all over the world there are more

accounts and stories of a heavenly war than are commonly known. One familiar report, easily obtainable, can be found in The Holy Bible's Old Testament book of Isaiah 14:12-15.

> 12. How art thou fallen from heaven, O Lucifer, son of the morning! How art thou cut down to the ground, which didst weaken the nations!
>
> 13. For thou hast said in thine heart, I will ascend into heaven, I will exalt my throne above the stars of God: I will sit also upon the mount of the congregation, in the sides of the north:
>
> 14. I will ascend above the heights of the clouds; I will be like the most High.
>
> 15. Yet thou shalt be brought down to hell, to the sides of the pit.

Cell Block Ice

As the exile story continues there is no more rebellion, no more to conquer, and no more war. Now Lucifer, Leviathan, and all of their co-conspirators have been cast back to where a portion of this delusional uprising began.

The earth had once been a peaceful place some of this rebel army first called home. But now home has become their prison. Earth, which was once lush and green, now lay destroyed because of the war. However, this planet is about to take on yet another transformation.

According to GOD'S will the ice age was brought about as an encasement for the rebellious angel and all his followers. Those evil beings were now held by cell blocks of ice in a snow-capped prison. These prisoners were securely placed so they could no longer cause any more harm or trouble.

Judgment fell once again as earth's frozen tundra became a maximum-security prison and holding place for a designated period of time. This action was not going to be GOD'S last decree for them. Their judgments from the Almighty had only just begun.

Thawed: Freedom from Restraints

At GOD'S discretion a specific time eventually arrived. The next phase would now begin to further implement the punishment of those fallen beings. Another judgment was to fall on the entire dark army.

Exercising authority with words of power, the Almighty called for an end to the ice age. Time now relegated to completing this command and eventually the ice became melted.

With the melting of earth's ice age the frozen prison eventually turned into a liquid wasteland. A watery flood now covered the entire earth. At the outset, this flood came about because one cocky angel believed he could out leverage and strong-arm GOD.

Lucifer's flood can prove evident though two different sources. The first piece of evidence presented will come from commonly known areas of science, history, and exploration. Extensive data has been collected from various sources proving the existence and melting of an ice age long ago here on earth. Even fossils of different creations were found from that period of time, proving other beings were once encased here on the planet.

The second source presented can also authenticate the event because it was GOD who had commanded this scenario to be brought about. In GOD'S *Word* it is seen where *"the earth was without form and void"* of any land mass here on the planet.

Now it can be applicable to take this pertinent data of the ice age flood waters and tie it back to the Old Testament reference previously used from Genesis 1:2. This verse must be looked at again literally in this new light.

> "And the earth was without form and void; and darkness was upon the face of the deep. And the Spirit of GOD moved upon the face of the waters."

Ponder the phrase *"darkness was upon the face of the deep"* for a moment. Could the *"darkness"* indicated here be exclusively referring to a state of environment, or are there further interpretations? Did this *"darkness"* also include the presence of Lucifer and his rebellious army?

Some may ask how that idea might be possible. Apparently, it would seem if GOD'S judgment of the ice age encapsulated those of a physical existence, then a thaw out could only produce deteriorated piles of decomposed bodies. And this is correct. Flesh, bone, and other matter would be destroyed.

To look further with a spiritual eye, it can be seen what happened to the cosmic criminals. Although the shell of the bodies had been destroyed, the individuals themselves had not. Entities that at one time existed as physical beings were now bound to survive here on earth in their spiritual forms only.

With the insightful information presented, might the *"darkness"* referred to in Genesis 1:2 also be a revelation for humanity? Does this verse present evidence pertaining to the physical release of a dark army from their jail cells constructed in ice? Was this a warning from GOD that a demonic host had been set free for further judgments on earth? For the skeptics these questions should not be ignored. For everyone who will listen to these words it should not be taken lightly that Lucifer, Leviathan, and their demonic hordes freely roam the earth we live on.

Chapter 2

GOD'S Declaration For Leviathan

GOD PROCLAIMED THROUGHOUT HIS *Word* numerous statements regarding the topic of an evil entity known as Leviathan. Some proclamations can be found in *The Holy Bible's* Old Testament book of Job.

These particular accounts of the crown prince are very important because the collective information presents a variety of warnings exposing the dangers of Leviathan. Those warnings found in the book of Job is undeniable truth, revealed by the Almighty, in order to educate humanity of a deadly enemy.

For a convenient reference Job chapter 41 has been provided. As a reminder this particular translation was recorded from the King James Version.

> 41:1. Canst thou draw out leviathan with an hook? or his tongue with a cord which thou lettest down?
>
> 41:2. Canst thou put an hook into his nose? or bore his jaw through with a thorn?
>
> 41:3. Will he make many supplications unto thee? will he speak soft words unto thee?

41:4. Will he make a covenant with thee? wilt thou take him for a servant for ever?

41:5. Wilt thou play with him as with a bird? or wilt thou bind him for thy maidens?

41:6. Shall the companions make a banquet of him? shall they part him among the merchants?

41:7. Canst thou fill his skin with barbed irons? or his head with fish spears?

41:8. Lay thine hand upon him, remember the battle, do no more.

41:9. Behold, the hope of him is in vain: shall not one be cast down even at the sight of him?

41:10. None is so fierce that dare stir him up: who then is able to stand before me?

41:11. Who hath prevented me, that I should repay him? whatsoever is under the whole heaven is mine.

41:12. I will not conceal his parts, nor his power, nor his comely proportion.

41:13. Who can discover the face of his garment? or who can come to him with his double bridle?

41:14. Who can open the doors of his face? his teeth are terrible round about.

41:15. His scales are his pride, shut up together as with a close seal.

41:16. One is so near to another, that no air can come between them.

41:17. They are joined one to another, they stick together, that they cannot be sundered.

41:18. By his neesings a light doth shine, and his eyes are like the eyelids of the morning.

41:19. Out of his mouth go burning lamps, and sparks of fire leap out.

41:20. Out of his nostrils goeth smoke, as out of a seething pot or caldron.

41:21. His breath kindleth coals, and a flame goeth out of his mouth.

41:22. In his neck remaineth strength, and sorrow is turned into joy before him.

41:23. The flakes of his flesh are joined together: they are firm in themselves; they cannot be moved.

41:24. His heart is as firm as a stone; yea, as hard as a piece of the nether millstone.

41:25. When he raiseth up himself, the mighty are afraid: by reason of breakings they purify themselves.

41:26. The sword of him that layeth at him cannot hold: the spear, the dart, nor the habergeon.

41:27. He esteemeth iron as straw, and brass as rotten wood.

> 41:28. The arrow cannot make him flee: slingstones are turned with him into stubble.
>
> 41:29. Darts are counted as stubble: he laugheth at the shaking of a spear.
>
> 41:30. Sharp stones are under him: he spreadeth sharp pointed things upon the mire.
>
> 41:31. He maketh the deep to boil like a pot: he maketh the sea like a pot of ointment.
>
> 41:32. He maketh a path to shine after him; one would think the deep to be hoary.
>
> 41:33. Upon earth there is not his like, who is made without fear.
>
> 41:34. He beholdeth all high things: he is a king over all the children of pride.

An Interpretation of Job

Within chapter 41 is a vast array of insights regarding the crown prince of the deep. Written in Job 41 are variations of questions, interjections, input, and divine enlightenment.

In comparing verses 1 and 2, some interesting questions are put forth. These questions seemingly ask the same thing. Is it possible for a human being, under their own natural strength, to somehow capture or take control of the great Leviathan? To paraphrase, how would it be humanly possible to take hold of such a supernatural

GOD'S Declaration For Leviathan

being with physical hands and bind him through a natural means?

As the chapter continues verses 3 and 4 solidify how the crown prince deliberates toward people. Those verses present important pieces of truth.

First, these particular words conclude that Leviathan, the sea-dragon, will never willingly submit himself under any human or human law. Also it is clearly seen where this mighty Archon would never work toward benefitting a single man, woman, or child.

It is quite the contrary. This enormous entity would do it's due diligence to consume anyone who tried to leverage any control over him.

The next few verses continue to describe more of Leviathan's genuine interactions with humanity. Through numerous questions more ideas are purposed within those words. However, to sum up the idea, this being cannot be constrained like a human pet and will never be tamed by our species in itself.

A bleak picture regarding a legitimate fight between any human being and Leviathan is painted in verses 8-10. Conveyed through these words, for a person to physically contemplate victory over the Archon would most likely be thoughts and efforts of vanity. So realistically any hope of someone naturally defeating Leviathan would seem useless.

This picture continues to reaffirm the questioning of who could be able to stand face-to-face with this sea-dragon and remain undefeated. Again, what human possesses the resilience to look directly at Leviathan and not *"be cast down"* in his presence? Or who *"is so fierce that dare stir him up"* for battle?

Continuing on, images are painted of the crown prince

in verses 18-22. Initially his eyes are described as brightly gleaming and blustery as the rising sun.

Next would be his mouth. When Leviathan opens his lips fire comes forth. Intensive flames are reported to *"leap out"* in an effort to consume whom it may. Apparently as the crown prince speaks, his words aim to devastate and devour.

In verse 20 it is stated that from *"his nostrils goeth smoke, as out of a seething pot or cauldron."* Evidently this individual exhales such a stout and overwhelming disillusionment that it physically can consume like smoke and vapor.

Verse 24 describes the condition of Leviathan's heart. The description will begin with the Archon's *"heart is as firm as a stone"* then adding this particular organ is *"as hard as a piece of the nether millstone."* Surely nothing good or kind could come from a being in such a condition.

A great honor is mentioned in verse 33 regarding Leviathan. In this verse it has been said that upon the *"earth there is not his like,"* alluding to the Archon's might and fortitude. There is no one on the planet like the crown prince of the deep. He is someone *"who is made without fear."*

Chapter 3

Leviathan's Realm

A PRESENCE OF LEVIATHAN can be felt almost anywhere on the earth, at any time, as the spiritual manifestation of this sea-dragon travels the planet's vast oceans and waterways. However, the Archon's dominion is not limited to a watery environment. His areas of authority transcend the mighty seas and are capable of operating proficiently on dry land as well.

Working hand in hand with his unseen minions and human subjects Leviathan operates a wide variety of realms abroad. There is not one continent, one country, nor one region on the globe where this crown prince does not have someone or something stationed and awaiting orders. Through precise motion he is able to personally supervise such a large area for Lucifer and the kingdom of darkness because the Archon can quickly transfer from one location to another.

In beginning to dive deep into some of these seen and unseen places, prepare yourself. Be prepared to witness the workings of Leviathan and those controlled by him. Be prepared to view the hidden snares placed by these realms belonging to the crown prince. Prepare to behold the utter horror people endure once the traps for their souls are sprung.

Go West

Throughout time there has always been a mysterious tugging on the human soul from the west. Many examples can be given. One such instance can date back to the 1800's and involves a yearning which came about for a variety of individuals on the American continent. The yearning held to a notion of a migration westward.

During this particular period various rumors circulated throughout numerous populations in the United States. Untold possibilities of land, adventure, and even gold were just a few of the enticements people heard of and sought after.

Exciting words of a new life and prosperity flowed from ear to ear. Many began to foster the illusions of setting their sights on becoming greater and more powerful. Although perilous dangers were spoken of as well in these travels, the warnings to most paled in comparison to the desire of securing a more comfortable tomorrow.

Of course there were a multitude of reasons people wanted to travel and settle in that direction. Many of those motives may have been directed toward good will and intent. But could there have also been other explanations why some were mesmerized and lured west? Was there something, or someone, tugging at the heartstrings of those willing to strike out at the unknown, no matter what it may cost them? If an unknown force was at work then, could this untold force be at work from the western hemisphere today?

Before these questions can be answered stemming from a supernatural viewpoint, a particular piece of information must be covered first. But before the piece of information is brought forth a warning must be issued.

That warning is a precaution to the dangerous realm about to be entered.

In this particular chapter, certain limited information of an occult nature will be referenced. The subject matter is only applicable to the topic at hand and solely mentioned as evidence to confirm the validity of the topic.

The insights are not presented to promote a reading of or exploration into occultism. Occultism is overwhelmingly destructive and should be considered the workings of the dark kingdom.

If there are any occult items, books, or propaganda in your home, it is recommended to properly dispose of these items as soon as possible. Every occult item made has had a demonic spirit assigned to that particular object or media. So by proxy, in allowing the items in your home has allowed an evil spirit there as well.

The particular piece of information to bring forth for this general topic will come from a book released in 1969, *The Satanic Bible*. Its author was Mr. Anton LaVey.

Although that particular book appears fashioned after the *Judeo-Christian Bible*, two major differences exist. The first and foremost important difference would be these two books were inspired by and purposed for two opposing sources.

The Holy Bible was, is, and always will be the divine recorded words and will of GOD, our Creator. That particular book is meant to restore and empower humanity once again supernaturally, and demonstrates how and why every person is able to obtain life eternal.

The Satanic Bible promotes illusions from the dark kingdom and ultimately propagates an ideology of the fallen angel Lucifer. The underlying efforts of that book are meant to confuse and deceive mankind, with an intention to ultimately bring a spiritually eternal death to every human being possible.

The second major difference between these two books are their physical authors. Instead of having numerous human penmen throughout centuries of time and sixty-six smaller books contained within its writings as the *Judeo-Christian Bible* does, *The Satanic Bible* had one penman and five chapters. One of these chapters in Mr. LaVey's book is entitled "Leviathan."

To give a basic overview, found within the Leviathan chapter is a particular element connected to the sea-dragon. The element of water is used in relation to this crown prince of the deep.

Also contained within that particular chapter is the general direction Lucifer bestowed upon Leviathan to reign over in the angel's absence. Leviathan continuously leads an assault against humanity from these earthly regions. The direction named is west, or the western hemispheric realms.

If the legitimacy of the information was to ever fall into question, all one would have to do is look at the confirming source. The author of *The Satanic Bible*, Mr. LaVey, possessed an in-depth and insightful understanding with regard to the layout of the kingdom of darkness. He was more than just an occult author and satanist of a minor degree. Mr. LaVey was a satanic priest, and commissioned by darkness to begin a church called the First Church of Satan.

Initially located in the western hemisphere of the United States, Mr. LaVey's church began its mission for darkness in San Francisco, California. After growing from a few members to over thousands, and the death of Mr. LaVey in 1996, spin-offs from the church began to spring up with headquarters established also in the western United States. Most notably were the Satanic Church and the Temple of Set.

With all this information brought into the light, let us return to those questions asked earlier in the chapter and look at them from a supernatural viewpoint. Back in the 1800's, could there have been other explanations as to why certain people were mesmerized and lured west?

The answer to the first question is yes.

Some in humanity may have been drawn west, in part, because Leviathan needed mankind to begin to populate and buildup a realm he had been placed over. This crown prince drew those he would easily lead to construct what he wanted. No matter what had to transpire, a multitude of land bases must be firmly established in the west for the kingdom of darkness.

The second question mirrors the first. Could there have been something, or someone, tugging at the heartstrings of those willing to strike out at the unknown, no matter what it may cost them?

The answer to the second question is yes.

Many things tugged at the hearts of those heading west, but not all were bad. A new life, a new experience, and the possibility to better oneself were certainly motivating factors. Also there were those who hoped to elevate the lives of people they cared for. Legitimately some people headed west for their families, loved ones, and future generations.

Nevertheless, there was also a tugging at others heartstrings by Leviathan and the kingdom of darkness. Humans had to be brought forth, controlled, and made a slave to do the will of the dark kingdom. Through various ploys many were convinced to believe anything just to bring them into the realms of Leviathan.

The third question is useful for today. If an unknown force was at work then, could this untold force be at work from the western hemisphere today?

Simply put the answer to that question is yes.

The Archon and his minions were hard at work back then. Just as they were in times past, these evil forces still work today to further mankind's destruction.

To examine the idea let's take a look at this concept from a practical view. Some of the most powerful influences and trends originate from the west. In the west there is Hollywood and the mainstream music business. In the west there is an abundance of pride: self-pride, gay pride, secular pride, and pride of every shape, size, and form. In addition, some of the largest and most well-known occult movements, religions, ideologies, and churches are located in the west.

What Leviathan and his minions had built back in the 1800's seemingly took hold. Today many human populations increase daily westward. And as more deception pours out to the masses, portions of the kingdom of darkness continue to grow larger and larger while this crown prince waves the banner "Go West."

Too Big To Fail

It should never be taken lightly that Leviathan's realm of haughtiness (or high-mindedness) is a deadly place within itself. Captivating and alluring, this particular realm can be easily accessible for anyone to enter. Admittance is truly a simple process.

One way to walk through that entrance can be by

idealistically promoting one's self in a godless way, such as fashioning puffed-up thoughts regarding what self can do, accomplish, or solely maintain. With that being said, let it also be stated that there are differences between Leviathan's haughtiness and a healthy human being's state of confidence.

Without question, there is nothing wrong with looking upon what one has completed and accomplished with satisfaction as long as the motives are right. In comparison that same act and type of behavior is recorded in *Scripture* of our Creator. Proof can be found in the Old Testament book of Genesis 1:31.

> "And God saw every thing that he had made, and behold, it was very good. And the evening and the morning were the sixth day."

Throughout the previous verses in chapter 1 of Genesis, GOD had finished recreating the earth from Lucifer's flood. After the recreation process HE looked back at what had been completed and thought, *"it was very good."* Therefore, if it were wrong or wicked to be happy about an accomplishment then GOD would not have exhibited the same behavior.

There is not a problem in saying job well done. An issue begins when someone's accomplishments have been blown out of proportion to the point where the feat itself becomes idolatrous within that person or people's existence.

The more any idol is focused upon, the more it will grow and manifest. And as idols continue to manifest themselves larger and larger without restraint, sin will ultimately consume those entangled in its web. To give an example of how this premise works in Leviathan's realm of haughtiness, a short story will follow after a brief acknowledgement.

In a published article dated April 15, 2019, Olivia Mason wrote that "Countless people have written about the subject," and this is ever so true. Numerous writers, explorers, and enthusiast have written secular fiction and non-fiction articles, books, plays, and even movies regarding the base subject matter for over a century. Some of the information gathered for this story, to give an accurate account, has come from a multitude of factual sources.

However, although infused with public facts and various accounts from different secular sources, this particular recollection of such a popular story will be told from a spiritual viewpoint.

The calendar date displayed March 31, 1909. There was a stir in the town of Belfast, because something big happened to be on the minds of many of the town's folk. People were talking back and forth as excitement could be felt just about everywhere. Today is the day the first keel plate would be laid in the construction of the great ship Titanic.

Certainly the Titanic deemed to be no ordinary ship made of steel. This particular ship was designed to be built as beautiful and luxurious as it would be strong, stout, and seaworthy. Reliability and dependability were to be its creed, as securable comfort became its motto and mission.

The Titanic had been laid out as a sizable ship of its caliber. None like it was ever seen. Because this ship would be so massive and unyielding, many of the builders and owners firmly believed that vessel would be virtually indestructible.

To speed up the story it is now May 31, 1911. What a special time indeed. Today is the day this great ship, the Titanic, will launch. Not only was the sea air flowing in the wind, but pride and loftiness filled the atmosphere.

Confidence flowed overtly high at the White Star Line Company. This was the company who made, owned, and operated the mammoth ship. Success of a great feat had at last been accomplished. What was once an idea with some blueprints had manifested into a colossal floating structure.

People were shaking hands, patting backs, and celebrating. Time finally arrived to congratulate each other on completing such a tremendous job and task. However, the story doesn't stop here. Leviathan secretly continued on the move and worked toward different plans for the humans.

This crown prince had prematurely imposed such high-minded attitudes within so many people in the company, that haughtiness and loftiness was afforded to run rampant. An environment developed in the project to the point that god-like attitudes became encouraged and promoted. Human mindsets were quickly getting out of hand with no restraints.

It had even been reported through numerous sources of one employee who went on record saying "Not even God himself could sink this ship." And as Leviathan took hold of various human hearts and minds many began to declare it openly and come in agreement with their words and deeds.

The crown prince experienced even further success in his campaign for destruction. Strongholds continued to develop in the hearts and minds of some of the intended victims. Sadly those mesmerized by the building of and strength of such a powerful vessel were still unaware of its weaknesses and vulnerabilities.

The day finally came. The date was April 10, 1912. The place, Southampton. Many who purchased their tickets stood in line to board this Goliath.

What a sizeable turnout. Even spectators showed up for the casting off because the voyage became highly publicized. Without any hesitations people throughout the crowd seemed high-spirited, chatty, and ready to experience the promise of a ride of their lives.

The lust of the flesh, the lust of the eyes, and the pride of life attacked a variety of individuals as they boarded this ship. Leviathan and his forces were everywhere, whipping up people in the frenzy of the moment. His task became easy. Not only was the size of the ship breathtaking to all its passengers, but the modern beauty and elegance of the vessel's internals seemed to some as a palace of royalty. The finest woods, the plushest carpets, and brass with chrome could be seen wherever you looked.

Also stored aboard the ship were the finest foods and beverages, along with enough champagne to flow all through the night. The evening menus were gourmet because all those who appeared on the "A" list must be catered to and given everything they want. Dancing and dining would take place into the wee hours of the morning. Then when it became time to wake from a festive evening, breakfast always awaited and was served in style. Of course, every planned lunch had to consist of something remarkable on its own.

Plans were made. The schedules set. Supplies

abundantly stocked and stored away. And as far as it was known every person's needs, wants, and desires could be taken care of at sea, or so it had been thought.

The ship set sail. Except for the initial near collision with the liner New York, everything seemed to be going off without a hitch. The Titanic headed to pick up more passengers and Queenstown was next on the schedule.

After taking on more people this massive ship continued on its way. Many individuals were dining, dancing, laughing, and experiencing the time of their lives. Most basked in the ambience, atmosphere, and excitement of the ride. But what was to come? Would Leviathan stand idly by and witness human beings having the time of their lives without interfering in the affairs of mankind?

The day is now April 14, 1912. A majority of those on this luxury ocean liner are still in celebration mode, unaware of the workings of Leviathan. That crown prince is about to further initiate a sadistic plan to begin drawing these unsuspecting victims into a cold watery trap aimed to catch their lives.

According to various references, around 1:40 p.m. the radio room of the Titanic receives an urgent message. This message is from the White Star ship Baltic. The Baltic is relaying a report from a Greek ship named the Athinai.

The Anthinai had broadcasted some important and hazardous information openly to all who will listen. That ship is letting all vessels in the area know they have encountered a large field of ice and numerous icebergs. The Baltic received the vital information and wanted to pass it on to everyone they could, including the Titanic.

These alarming words and warning quickly passed to the Titanic's Captain, Captain Edward J. Smith. Captain

Smith, who was also known as the Millionaire's Captain, reportedly did not take the warning seriously. On the contrary, he exhibited a lackluster attitude toward the news. Eventually that vital written message became waded up, stuck in a pocket, and left there until after 7 p.m. or so. Cleverly could this action have transpired through a smug tactic of the crown prince of the deep?

At 7:30 p.m., the Titanic's radio room intercepted another warning. These words were from the ship Antillian. That ship warned all who would listen they had spotted some icebergs and gave the coordinates. Immediately the information was reported to the bridge, but would the cautioning words to a potentially harmful situation be ignored from yet another vessel at sea?

Once again Captain Smith could not be found at his command post on the bridge. A junior officer had been assigned to the position and entrusted with the welfare of this massive vessel, so it fell to him how to handle these perilous words. Without any delay the vital information easily slipped right through the cracks. Apparently, step by step, Leviathan kept reeling the Titanic into his deadly trap.

For a brief moment Captain Smith returned to the ship's bridge. Upon exiting the bridge a little after 9 p.m. the Captain left word to let him know if he were needed.

Leviathan's influence had been hard at work on the Captain and crew. How else could it be explained why the Captain did not stay at his post, especially at a crucial time for the ship? Captain Smith and the leadership had been made aware of all the warnings of ice and icebergs spotted by other ships in the area on this day. But something, or someone, kept these men thinking and

Leviathan's Realm

believing that nothing could stand in the way of their massive ship.

It's past 9:30 p.m. and the Titanic's radio room received yet another broadcast regarding a lot of ice and numerous icebergs. This time it was the ship Mesaba.

The radio room operator at that specific time wrote down yet more words of impending danger. But because so many other warnings regarding the same subject matter had been reported throughout the day, this message from the Mesaba was again not taken seriously. Leviathan seemingly had convinced many aboard the Titanic everything would be safe and secure. Nevertheless, things were about to change and take a turn for the worst.

A little over two hours later something altered the course of the Titanic. Instead of smooth sailing while everyone either dined, danced, or slept under the bright mood night, a startling event suddenly began to unfold. Ice of a great magnitude seemed to emerge from nowhere. Suddenly the frozen substance appeared everywhere in a moment of time. Now it became evident that the ship found itself in a minefield of ice and danger.

Then the unimaginable happened. At 11:40 p.m., on Sunday April 14, 1912, an iceberg and this huge seaworthy vessel called the Titanic collided. Right away the ship experienced heavy damage as steel plates began buckling in its hull. While the plates were crushing and began to separate, sea water filled the ship once believed to be unsinkable.

The initial jolt of hitting something in the deep sea did not seem to panic many on board at first. Ideally this had been, after all, a ship most people were deceived into believing could not sink and was way too big to fail. The standing joke, until now, still circulated of "a ship God himself could not sink." But soon there would be no time for jokes.

As the alarms blasted through the speakers, a rise of confusion began to concern those aboard the luxury liner. Within a matter of time water filled the inward areas of the ship and this mammoth vessel began to sink. All initial hope transformed into despair, and the orders passed down to abandon ship.

Quickly passengers were herded toward the lifeboat stations in an attempt to begin saving lives. All of a sudden the haughtiness of Leviathan's lies and deceptions began to surface as the untouchable ship began to sink. SOS was now the call of the morning.

People of all walks of life were running here and there. As more individuals gathered together on deck, it became obvious some type of organized emergency evacuation needed to be put into working order. Although struggling to maintain any orderly structure, confusion swept the hearts of many of those who were on a ship which claimed untouchable by GOD.

If things were not chaotic enough there was another problem. The ship had not been supplied with the adequate amount of lifeboats to help all the passengers, crew, and officers escape off a seemingly watery steel coffin.

Regardless of the inadequacies, what lifeboats were available began to be filled with people then lowered into a cold and careless Atlantic Ocean. Uncertainty and fear began to grasp at these helpless individuals who minutes earlier were on a sinking ship. Then, with crushed spirits and only a will to survive, those on board these little boats beheld a terrible sight.

These survivors witnessed this steel vessel sinking

into the depths of its watery grave. Images and sounds were everywhere as people screamed, cried, and wailed for help. The cold waters splashed to and fro while many left stranded on the ship tried to swim to safety. But safety could be found nowhere, because there were more people than spaces in the life rafts.

The unforgiving coldness of the Atlantic had no mercy. Its waves felt no remorse for all who would fall prey to the chilling effects. Hypothermia began to set in quickly on those who were stranded in the water, as the dark depths began to claim those trapped by it.

On this day Leviathan's realm of haughtiness would claim many a human soul. On this day, the crown prince received into his domain those who fell for his trap and were deceived with his deadly lies.

As the mammoth-sized ship disappeared into the cold, dark, watery abyss, so did any fish tale, or challenge, of something so great that GOD could not touch. Leviathan had lured and deceived many people into putting themselves and their loved-ones in harm's way through cursing the vessel they were counting on. The curse had been accomplished when the Archon used certain people to openly challenge GOD that HE was not powerful enough to affect a piece of man-made property: the Titanic. And as Leviathan openly and unapologetically challenged GOD, GOD openly replied and gave a response that will forever be written down in the history of mankind.

LOOK

Leviathan operates freely and easily in the extreme realm of vanity. This crown prince and his minions actively strive in doing whatever is necessary to bring a person, or people, into a particular place of self-exaltation.

See who I am (prideful), look at my image (vanity), and the I, I, I, (self-centeredness) mentality are some good indicators to determine that someone is possibly coming under the influence of the Archon. The fore-mentioned ideologies can reflect like warning signals, giving an indication that Leviathan or one of his agents may be at work within the life of those who believe and function as such.

There is, however, nothing wrong with acknowledging one's abilities and gifting from the Almighty. GOD bestows unto every person various gifts, talents, or abilities. Therefore, everyone has something special and unique about him or her.

Furthermore, to recognize something wonderful about yourself and gratefully realize it is a gift from above is assuredly good in the eyes of our Creator.

Issues arise when agents from the crown prince are able to entice individuals with looking at their wonderful gifts, talents, and abilities, while forgetting and denying who indeed gave them those gifts. At that stage Leviathan can easily begin to slip a hook in his intended victim's mouth, as they look solely upon themselves and not toward the One who created them.

To give some idea how simple it is for Leviathan to accomplish his goal, a metaphorical story will be told. Although the characters in this story are fictional, the example of how the crown prince can operate is fact.

The story will begin in the deep southern United States, westward of Atlanta, Georgia. Found in a small rural community near such a thriving metropolis of people was one particular family. This growing family seemed to be ordinary with a dad, mom, and two small children.

The family appeared typical to the natural eye and blended in with their surroundings, all but one that is. The youngest girl had a gift of beauty. Her name was Susan.

From day one she was a beautiful little baby. And as she grew Susan blossomed like a rose.

Everywhere the family went together someone seemingly commented on how pretty Susan was. These comments usually made her parents very proud, while her older sister ignored the words. Susan's older sister had a nice appearance but was never praised like her younger sibling.

As Susan went through school those looks helped pave a way of ease. Because of her beauty Susan was always popular and accepted by almost every peer. Without much effort she won any contest she participated in. The girl also held many titles throughout school such as prom queen, fall harvest queen, and the most likely to succeed.

One time Susan's appearance even handed her student body president, simply because it seemed easy to be captivated by such a beautiful girl. And while all eyes were to be set on this young lady, there would be more than humans staring at Susan. Evidently aids of Leviathan had their eyes peering toward her from afar.

Before graduating from high school Susan faced the dilemma of what professional path to take. Her dad was a firefighter and her mom a nurse. Susan's parents chose these careers because they both wanted to help other people. Now it became time for Susan to make her decision, but would she choose her own future or would Leviathan decide it for her?

Susan narrowed her choices down to two prospects. First and foremost happened to be the medical field, just like her mother. This path was considered because many times Susan showed she had a big heart and really wanted to help others. Susan also wanted to be like her mother.

For one reason or another Susan always felt drawn back to her own beauty, so becoming a model as some of her friends suggested came in second place.

Her parents advised their daughter to apply to a variety of colleges and schools in both fields. On their advice she did just that.

Surprisingly in quick fashion she received an acceptance letter to both a medical college and a modeling school. Susan knew she could not go to both institutes. One offer had to be accepted and one offer had to be declined. What choice would she make, and which way would her life go?

Susan seemed to be mentally torn about what to do. She knew the medical field would help others and be a more secure future, whereas learning to model could be glamorous and exciting. While struggling with what decision to make, Leviathan began to whisper words into her ears and nudge the unsuspecting teen in the direction he wanted for her life.

After some overshadowing influence from the crown prince and covert leverage from those he sent to speak into her life, Susan decided to take up modeling. This girl had been reaffirmed enough that she had the looks and body for such a career. And while Susan thought she had received an offer to attend a modeling school in New

York because of her gift of beauty and charm, the young lady had in fact taken the bait laid out by Leviathan's agents.

Without much thought Susan hastily moved to New York. The fast pace of the new environment seemed to stretch her at first. While she was being stretched and dazzled by the lights and sounds of the big city, the sea-dragon began to initiate the next stage in his diabolical plan for her life.

Right away school and work seemed to consume Susan's every waking moment. When she wasn't in school she would be at work. Without reservation the reality of life began to set in as well as some exhaustion. But this was only the beginning of her busy and chaotic schedule, as the crown prince implemented his next phase.

One day while at school she was reminded by agents of Leviathan that she wasn't the prettiest face in the room anymore. These spirits kept pointing out to her that girls from all over the world attended this school. Their words went on and on of how beautiful, elegant, and charming the competition seemed to be.

In the same time-frame the crown prince made another strategic move and brought Sharee across her path. It wasn't common knowledge that Sharee was a disciple of Leviathan's, but she served him well. This creature of beauty held a power that could captivate the eyes as well as the soul. Because of that power Sharee and Susan were drawn together almost instantly.

Sharee's assignment from the crown prince began with her strategy to befriend Susan and gain the girl's confidence. Once successful in that endeavor, the next stage of the plan would be to guide Susan down a dark and crooked path, a path on which Leviathan and his minions awaited. These were her orders and what Sharee set out to do.

After befriending the unsuspecting girl Sharee began to plant little ideas in Susan's mind and thought process. The job needed to be the first thing to go. Her employment had to disappear right away, because Susan must be stripped from any support not controlled by Leviathan.

Sharee attempted to convince Susan a career in modeling should be considered more important than anything else. She kept conveying to Susan the job seemed to drain all her energies. A lot of emphasis had also been placed on the fact that without the time commitment to her work schedule Susan could spend more time learning the ins and outs of how to be a professional model.

While Sharee's soft and encouraging words flowed from her lips to Susan's ears, these were the words the crown prince wanted this persuadable young lady to hear.

Without hesitation Susan spoke up. She stated how easy it would be to quite work and devote all her time to modeling, but there was one problem. The young lady had to work in order to pay for rent, food, and her other necessities.

After she had finished speaking Sharee gave a quick reply. "Go ahead and quit. You can live here with me and it won't cost you anything yet. You'll just repay me once you become a famous model."

After hearing these words Susan jumped for joy. The young lady felt she was going to be somebody famous. Now Susan thought nothing could get in her way.

She quickly went to get her belongings. Conveniently Susan's roommate, Jill, would be gone to work. After packing up her things she reached for the phone to call Jill and inform her about the move. Words from Leviathan whispered "forget her, you are off to a better life."

Susan paused for a minute. Then she convinced herself of not having enough time to talk right now. Effortlessly the young lady gathered her things and left the apartment without as much as leaving a note or saying goodbye.

Unopposed Susan dashed to the next stop. She walked into her place of employment and collected the last paycheck. As she began to walk toward the boss's office in order to inform him of her decision, more words were whispered into these unguarded ears by invisible forces.

"Why tell them anything. After all, you got what you came for. Look at it this way, one day you are going to be a star." These were the words and counsel Susan heard and listened to.

She suddenly stopped right in her tracks and turned toward the exit. Susan walked out the door and left the building without saying a word to anyone else.

After finishing these few errands she headed back to Sharee's as fast as possible. And as she completed the task of rearranging her life, spiritual waves from Leviathan continued to push her on.

Sharee had been successful in guiding Susan with some bad advice. However, it wasn't over yet. The loss of her job and self-sufficient ways were just the beginning. It was the beginning of things that would be taken from Susan.

She moved into Sharee's guest bedroom. Susan thought it kind of Sharee to offer her such a nice place to stay while continuing to study in modeling school, but she was mistaken. Now this agent of darkness had Susan unknowingly right where Leviathan wanted her.

Because Sharee also taught a class or two at the modeling school she and Susan interacted together almost all the time. You would not usually see one alone for long without the other one appearing from somewhere. Outwardly it seemed as if Sharee had taken Susan under her wing, but where was she really taking the young lady?

Soon Susan's lifestyle transformed to school during the day and a party or gathering somewhere with Sharee every night. The investment into a successful model's image was no small amount, but there weren't any worries. Leviathan's army secretly supplied Sharee with everything she needed for Susan. Overtly while things on the surface seemed to be top of the world for now, something else lurked beneath.

The next day Sharee and Susan were talking. Leviathan's agent wasted no time and began interjecting various thoughts into this teen's mind that a lifestyle of a model is very competitive. She cleverly pointed out that a successful model must take every opportunity available to be at the top of the industry.

Sharee tactfully brought up the fact that many famous models in the past, and even some presently in the limelight, have had some type of cosmetic or reconstructive surgery to enhance their looks. She said there was nothing wrong or illegal about it. Continuing on Sharee shared a secret that she, herself, had experienced a nip and a tuck here and there.

At first Susan, who now went by Suzette, thought only unattractive or disfigured people received those types of surgeries. However, after hearing what Sharee said she began to ponder the thoughts. The young lady began to imagine what she may look like with a little smaller nose, a higher cheekbone, or fuller lips. While her imagination became opened up to newer possibilities, Leviathan further inserted the hook to reel Susan in.

After pondering these many thoughts Suzette spoke up. She said different surgeries may give her an edge over the competition, but the cost was something she couldn't afford yet.

Even with Leviathan's grip tightening on her Suzette still saw herself as a model in training. Furthermore, recounting life's circumstances she acknowledged there might not be a place to live, or food to eat, without Sharee's help.

With no hesitation Sharee told Suzette she would happily back a new sensation. Sharee stated she knew a surgeon who did wonders, and could give him a call when the young model wanted her to.

Bombarded by heavy influences from the crown prince Suzette decided to have a reconstructive operation. The call was made and the surgery time set.

Within days her nip and tuck had been completed. Customarily there was a specific time allotted to heal. After the healing process Suzette seemed to begin standing out even more.

Somehow through the whole process Leviathan had penetrated the young lady's thoughts and way of thinking. Instead of depending on her natural beauty, working hard, training, and making the right connections, Suzette was shown a shortcut. She had been shown a shortcut where a nip, tuck, or injection could make all the difference.

Suzette started to receive many offers for modeling,

which in turn allowed her to make some good money. Instead of taking the money and becoming more independent the young lady continued to live with Sharee. She had been encouraged to stay because Sharee did not want her to go anywhere. The assignment had not been completed yet.

By now Suzette also obsessed with a consistent motivation to become more and more beautiful, so that is what she set out to do. Instead of enjoying the success handed to her and investing or saving what she earned, this individual's thoughts were led to believe more and more surgeries must be the way to go. A call to vanity had tugged and tugged at her until it became a strong addiction.

With repetition surgery after surgery took place in her life. Eventually, this once naturally beautiful person went through so many operations there were not many parts of her face and body which escaped the knife.

Then one day, after yet another surgery, she woke up and looked in the mirror. The face and image staring back at Suzette was not her own. Even though most of the young lady's body may have held up through all the reconstruction her appearance seemed so artificial looking. It had come to the point that with so many surgeries to her face Suzette now looked more like a creature than a beautiful model.

Because her looks were so transformed due to a faith in plastic surgery, Suzette began to lose a lot of work. Not only did she stop working, but in the industry she had become the story of what not to do.

Heavily depressed and out of money, hope, and friends, Suzette turned to the one person she had come to rely on so much: Sharee. But by now Sharee had almost completed her assignment from the crown prince. There was only one thing left for her to set into motion and see that it followed through.

Sharee went off unmerciful on Suzette, telling her what a mistake it was to have taken this inexperienced person under her wings. Sharee screamed all kind of hateful and hurtful things, insinuating Suzette would be nothing but a wash-up and has-been. That agent of Leviathan went on to say she wished she had never met this young student, and Susan, or Suzette, was no longer welcome in her home.

A long silent pause occurred for a minute or two. Suzette was then given until morning to vacate the premises or she would be thrown out in the street with her belongings.

The next morning Sharee went and knocked on Suzette's door. There was no answer and the doorknob locked. Sharee began screaming out profanities and banged on the door, but still no answer. She finally went and found a key to unlock the door.

What she found inside the room pleased her and her master Leviathan. Suzette had been lied to and placed under so much stress that she just laid there with an empty bottle, once full of pills, clutched in her hand. Suzette seemed lifeless as her cold body showed no motion and produced no breathe.

The snare of Leviathan in the realm of vanity caught its prey. The traps he set for this unsuspecting young individual were effective every time. And now he had won the final victory in Susan's life. Now he would have possession of her eternal soul forever.

The Next Generation

Contrary to what some may think, this crown prince places a high value on the human family orientation. Leviathan takes pleasure in one generation passing on a legacy to another, as long as that legacy is contained within his realms of thinking, logic, and understanding.

The Archon understands his cause is placed to a great advantage in this war with mankind if he is able to subjugate and dominate a human generation whom then procreates. The ideology behind the strategy is if the crown prince already controls an environment where human children are born into and trained, it will make the task of infiltrating and programming the next generation of his enemy (humanity) much easier to do.

Once the process has begun and proves successful in one age bracket, spirits of Leviathan will continue to grow and strengthen from generation to generation. His doctrines and ideologies will be undoubtedly handed down from parents to children.

To demonstrate how this particular premise can be accomplished, and how Leviathan can effect a family if he is permitted to influence them from generation to generation, a short metaphorical story will follow. Although the characters in this story are fictional, the example of how the crown prince operates in this type of setting is factual.

The story will begin with a lady named Hazel. "See, I told you so. Now let me have it so I can do it right" were the words Hazel aggressively spoke again to one of her children. She really didn't make any extra effort to be so harsh and crude, because that behavior had been instilled into her very nature.

Hazel acted either rude, insensitive, unfeeling, or overbearing most of the time, and not just with immediate family. One of the fore-mentioned behaviors could be seen taking place between her with most of the people she encountered. Hazel conducted herself in such a way because this was how the poor woman had been brought up from childhood. But let us start the story from an earlier beginning.

From an outward appearance Hazel's family of origin seemed to be an average family with a dad, mom, and three siblings. Both of her parents genuinely loved all their children the best they knew how. But even with all the attempted good intentions their family had some serious underlying problems.

Hazel's dad was a very stern person. The man always acted harsh and tough as they come. Eventually he became a physical abuser to his family as well.

Her mother possessed a gentle soul before she married. As time went on and because of all the abuse from her husband, Hazel's mom was emotionally and psychologically forced to change. The woman eventually developed into a shell of a person.

Through all the trauma this little girl had been subjected to, one could easily understand why Hazel acted the way she did. The children were made to show strength and not weakness when they were growing up or else risk suffering the wrath of a tyrant. Heaven forbid if these kids ever demonstrated any type of emotion.

The lifestyle surrounding Hazel was completely dysfunctional. No one in the family ever sought any type of help or counseling for their problems. Life seemed normal as far as her dad believed, and that would just be the way it was going to be for everyone else.

As the children grew old enough to leave home they did. Each one of them loved their mother dearly and tried to stay in contact with her. Their dad had become something else. He had been the whole reason his children ran from the home they knew and fled into other lives far from him.

Time had come for Hazel to leave home for college. She was only able to go to college because her grandparents helped pay for the tuition and books. What they were not able to help with Hazel had to cover herself, and she did.

Hazel had been trained to show no weakness and function as a very independent person, in part, because of how she was raised. Because of that training she went blasting through life with nothing to hold her back. Once the girl even had to work two jobs for a short time while in school but did not complain.

The date arrived as Hazel graduated with high marks, even making the Dean's List. This self-accomplished person was so proud of what she had achieved. Grasping her degree in one hand Hazel began to march on life. But would the graduate be in step with her own ambitions or someone else's?

By the time she was ready to leave her mid-western college Hazel had already been offered a couple of jobs. One job turned out to be near where her parents lived. The other job offer came from a company located on the west coast.

Hazel felt excited about the offer of two different jobs. The first offer, only a short drive from her parents, would be a good job. She knew the area, had a friend who already lived nearby, and was very familiar with that side of town.

Then the lady calculated how her dad lived close by as well. Hazel knew if she lived there he would never stop meddling in her life. He would be the type of person to never leave things alone.

On that one thought of her dad's intrusiveness Hazel decided to accept the second offer thousands of miles away. Right away she packed her bags and began the journey west.

Even though their parting had only been a few hours before, the young individual soon began to miss her mother. Seemingly as quick as she felt the longing for her absent mother, Hazel began to emotionally experience the anticipation of her new life on the coast. Excitement could be felt in the air as thoughts swirled around and around. Was the churning just a thrill of a new life, or would it be the whirling of something more supernatural, like Leviathan?

Evidently the crown prince of the deep already held a secure place somewhere within this person's heart, because he successfully acquired room within her very soul from a youthful age. It was obvious that Leviathan's presence would easily be attached to Hazel's every move. It had to be, because the sea-dragon had been first allowed into her dad's life and soul.

Leviathan continued with an overwhelming attempt to guide Hazel's movements. He tried to direct many choices she made, as this person stayed unknowingly unaware of his looming presence and influence. Eventually the crown prince had ingrained himself so much in the girl's mentality that in reality he began to call all the shots for her life.

Now that Leviathan seemingly had no resistance controlling Hazel rationally, he could begin to interject more of his will for her. Without obstructions the crown prince would further begin to manifest his true intentions for the young lady's future.

In no time she settled into her new job and life. Because of her fieriness and go get it attitude, Hazel started to quickly advance within the company. At the same time her business life began to take off so did Hazel's personal life.

At the office this young lady met a nice, easy going young man named Tom. Tom showed a lot of kindness and gentleness toward Hazel, and that she adored. He was the kind of guy she really liked, in part, because Tom displayed something totally opposite from her dad. He demonstrated compassion and kindness.

The couple began to date, then moved to seeing each other quite often. One thing continued to lead to another. Within eight months of dating the two became engaged to be married.

When it came time to make the wedding plans Tom thought about a big, beautiful wedding. He wanted to show off his new bride to the world in style. However, Hazel had other plans.

Through the fear and anxiety of having to invite her dad she persuaded Tom to have a small wedding. So that was what they did. The couple had a small wedding with just a few close friends.

Time went on. The couple had two small children together. Hazel's career also continued to skyrocket. At this point she had earned a promotion to a position of authority high atop the company.

The new COO had proven to many that she was a dedicated, career-minded woman. Hazel also believed just because she had children did not mean it would be her responsibility to nurse them along in life. On the contrary, this lady had been raised to be strong, and toughness was what Hazel determined to pass on to the next generation.

Because she had rapidly advanced to such a high degree and was doing so well, Hazel decided it would be more financially feasible for Tom to cut back his work schedule and supervise the children instead of her. Hesitantly Tom listened to his wife and eventually set out to do what she asked.

When he approached his boss regarding the cut back to part-time, Tom found out company policy in that particular department would not allow it. His position had full-time responsibilities designed for one person to handle, not numerous people.

In light of the information and because he had also promised her, Tom stuck to the original plan Hazel (and Leviathan) came up with. He told the supervisor if it were not possible to go to part-time he could no longer work there. Tom was let go.

On the way home Tom began to think of how his wife would respond to what happened with the job. When he arrived Hazel was already there because she had gotten off early. As Tom told her everything the news didn't seem to be bothersome at all.

Surprisingly the woman insinuated that this is actually good news. Hazel wasted no time to quickly boast "With the salary I make, there will still be enough money for my family to live a real good life, so no sweat there." After this statement the environment became filled with a variety of emotions.

When the initial shock wore off from these cold and seemingly brash words Tom spoke up. Without any reservation he wanted to find another job, even if it were only part-time.

However, through the influences of the crown prince Hazel immediately said no. And as it had always been in their relationship, whatever Hazel wanted and desired would happen without resistance.

Right away things began to change around the couple's home. The first decision Hazel made, after rearranging Tom's life how she wanted it, was to fire the nanny. She felt since Tom no longer held a public job he could be responsible for keeping up with the home and taking care of the children full-time. Submitting to her wishes he complied.

Leviathan and his minions continued to guide Hazel from one decision to another, ever increasingly positioning her authority and control over the family. The crown prince instructed her in everything he desired for Hazel to do. Through listening to those voices from the deep, she had become the sole breadwinner and main decision maker for four human beings.

By Leviathan empowering Hazel to be head of the household and pulling her strings, he cleverly placed himself in a great position. The Archon had been placed in a position to be lord over their household, lord over each of their lives, and lord over their future.

With all that he had cunningly accomplished Leviathan became successful with his endeavors regarding this family. First he had Hazel and the deep parts of her soul. Then he covertly positioned himself to rule over Tom and have that man knuckled down through Hazel's actions and dysfunctional attitudes. Finally the crown prince obtained something he had aimed for from the beginning. Now there was another generation of humans he could influence and control by being there for Hazel's children as he had been there for her through her dad.

Chapter 4

Leviathan's Power

LEVIATHAN HAS CONTINUOUSLY demonstrated throughout time that he is a powerful being. Easily the crown prince can call upon a variety of abilities and weaponry which are at his disposal. Undeniable the Archon's shrewd discipline allows him to effectively exercise these certain abilities and weapons of war against the lives of men, women, and children everywhere.

The purpose and goal of this spiritual war is crystal clear to the sea-dragon. There is an objective to ultimately gain possession of as many human souls for the kingdom of darkness as possible. So bear witness to a few of the many ways Leviathan flexes his muscles and ability for accomplishing conquest and domination over humanity.

Arrogance:
A Reasoning Behind Disaster

One way this crown prince will attempt to bring the masses under his influence and control is through the power of arrogance. Arrogance can simply begin as conscience or subconscious thoughts ushered in by the Archon or one of his agents.

Eventually certain thoughts may turn into ideas. If those reverberating ideas are not reigned in it is a good possibility they could resonate into beliefs. Once a strong enough belief occurs an ideology will soon develop. It is those well-crafted ideologies which possess an overwhelming power to be all consuming.

For example, look at the "greater than thou art" ideology. This particular ideology has existed since the fall of the cosmos. While there were those then whom saw themselves as better than everyone else, seemingly whether in secret or openly the concept still effectively runs rampant throughout the world today.

GOD views arrogance as something deadly and destructive for humanity to be entangled with. The topic is so important that there have been numerous verses placed in *The Holy Bible* to cover the destructive force of arrogance.

One of these verses can be found in the Old Testament book of 1 Samuel chapter 2, in the first half of verse 3.

> "Talk no more so exceeding proudly; let not arrogancy come out of your mouth:"

This portion of the verse not only issues clear instruction, but also gives a warning to not speak or believe arrogantly. GOD knew if human beings gave any room for arrogance, we, in fact, would be giving room in our lives to Leviathan. Without a doubt once the Archon has been cleverly positioned anywhere within a person's life, chaos and destruction will eventually follow.

To give an eerie example of the effects concerning Leviathan's influential power of arrogance, a story will follow. The story is true, also one of sadness. The story is recorded throughout the pages of history, clearly demonstrating what can occur if the crown prince is allowed to direct our lives and the lives of those we love, cherish, or care for.

History books can date back to July 29, 1945. Somewhere in the Philippine Sea sat a United States naval war vessel, the U.S.S. Indianapolis. The ship and its crew just completed a top-secret assignment, a mission which eventually would assist in ending World War II.

New orders were issued and now it was time for the crew to set sail toward the next assignment. Before their departure, the Captain of the ship, Charles B. McVay, checked-in with Naval Operations. A request was made at that time to see if any escort ships were available to accompany the Indianapolis to its new assignment.

Reportedly command replied that no escort ships were necessary. How odd such a viable request being denied in a time of war. Was this really the reply of rational and logical thinking human beings trained for war, or could the response ultimately have been made by the influences and workings of Leviathan?

As a single warship with no escort vessel to assist them through any unknown or perilous dangers they may encounter at sea, the Indianapolis had to depend on themselves instead of the command they served under. These brave sailors and marines did not waiver because of setting sail alone. On the contrary, these men girded themselves up and began to undertake another assignment in ending the bloodshed in the South Pacific.

With the ship and its crew having a unified goal of service to country it was full steam ahead. There may have been those who believed the more expedient their assignments were accomplished the sooner the war would end. Although most sea-hardened warriors aboard the ship this night felt ready for a fight, many a man surely longed for peace or held thoughts of loved-ones back home close to their heart.

Around midnight a startling event occurred. The sizeable ship physically came under a surprise attack of some kind. It had been without warning that an entity from nowhere suddenly struck a devastating blow.

Danger apparently arrived from an unexpected agent of the dark depths, as a Japanese submarine launched a torpedo and made a solid hit. Now this thirteen-year-old ship might be in for some serious trouble, because the extensive severity of the problem at that moment remained in question. Another good question would be did Leviathan make certain moves through others he controlled, in order to have these men and their ship positioned right where he wanted them?

Quickly damage assessments were gathered regarding the ship. Not long after these assessments were made it became evident the powerful vessel was headed for the bottom.

Orders went out instructing a distress signal to be broadcast for any to hear. These men on this once mighty ship needed help, and they needed it now.

The signal had indeed been heard by some, but immediately Leviathan's agents began their workings and mesmerized the minds of those who heard the call for help. Through arrogance and strategic mind-manipulation the distress call was disregarded and went without any response.

Back on the ship while chaos and everything else seemed to be happening all at once, some hard decisions must be made right away. When he knew without a doubt the ship was going to sink, Captain McVay thought about his men and passed on the orders. Now had become the time to abandon ship.

The crew of the Indianapolis implemented their Captain's command. Many began the process of abandoning the sinking vessel ever how they could. Some used a makeshift lifeboat or only had enough time to physically jump overboard. Others were thrown from the ship (like Captain McVay) because of numerous explosions and the ship wrenching as it began to break apart and sink.

Of a crew almost counting 1,200 people, it was reported that about 850 or so men initially made it off the ship and into the water alive. They were alive, but many were wounded, hurt, or dismayed when they hit the deep blue.

Everyone was going into survival mode. Staying alive and helping others live became the only objective. But most of these men who survived this attack of war were placed to a fate worse than the mercy of their human enemies or the sea. They were placed at the mercy of Leviathan.

Unceasingly the crown prince continued an attack on these berated souls. The rising smell of death, blood, and fear began to fill the air.

Leviathan attacked these men from every angle he could. He attacked their mentality and ability. He attacked their psychology and fortitude. He attacked their determination and drive. The sea-dragon even had them physically attacked by his fleshly minions from the depths of the ocean.

It was 850 or so men who survived the initial attack

and sinking of the Indianapolis. Of the 850 survivors who made it alive to the water, only 318 of those men were eventually rescued some four days later when they were pulled from their impending watery graves.

On and off the seas Leviathan aided in bringing about an event so shattering the story would never be forgotten. He brought about an event that painfully touched the lives of so many for generations to come.

In his book *The Pacific Campaign*, author Dan van Vat wrote in regard to the U.S.S. Indianapolis "she had been allowed out alone because the Americans had written off the Japanese Navy as a threat in the rear areas." Could this travesty have taken place because of Leviathan's power of arrogance and all the high-minded misinformation he placed over certain key individuals in positions of power, authority, and decision-making? Were there realistically certain people the crown prince mesmerized with deception and used as pawns in his deadly game?

Was the attack truly something orchestrated from the pits of hell? If so, could there have been a reason for the retaliation? Might it have had something to do with the ship and crew's previous assignment which eventually aided in bringing to an end such a bloody and senseless war; a war actively destroying many in the human race? Is there a possibility that ultimately it is the fault of Leviathan and his minions for the sinking of the U.S.S. Indianapolis?

Which Way Will I Go?

The Assyrian city of Nineveh seemed to be more than just a thriving town. This metropolis had many events taking place within its borders and rightfully so. What else could be expected with a city of almost 120,000 people living in it.

However, there was something other than its size and commerce that gave Nineveh such a well-known reputation. That place had been all-encompassed by an overwhelming wickedness, a darkness which seemingly held the lands. An outpouring of evil could be felt even into the atmosphere as the environment became completely saturated in such an eerie feeling of pride.

The Creator of heaven and earth looked down from a celestial throne room and beheld this populated city. Witnessing Nineveh's wickedness because the kingdom of darkness had consumed the city's people, GOD decided something would be done about it. The time for action was now.

Instead of wiping away the presence of darkness by simply eradicating these sinful human beings from the lands HE created, the Creator had a different plan. Something else would take place. GOD chose to first give grace and mercy instead of judgment.

It had been determined to send a man named Jonah unto the inhabitance of Nineveh. Jonah was delegated to bring these people an apparent word from the Almighty. GOD wanted a warning sent for those human beings who were drowning in darkness before it became too late for their souls.

Clear evidence proving Jonah's divine commission is recorded in *The Holy Scripture's* Old Testament book of Jonah 1:1-2.

> 1. Now the word of the LORD came unto Jonah the son of Amittai, saying,
>
> 2. Arise, go to Nineveh, that great city, and cry against it; for their wickedness is come up before me.

After the heavenly command had been issued Jonah questioned why GOD would send him to help Assyria, Israel's enemy. Surely the patriotic Jewish man felt some internal struggles and prejudices regarding the Assyrians and their city of Nineveh. While Jonah wrestled within himself over these orders, Leviathan began to grasp a deadly grip around this chosen messenger from GOD.

With reservations Jonah arose and prepared to set out on a journey. There were, however, thoughts in the air of what needed to be done. Would the servant of GOD obey the orders, or did this man have something else possibly on his mind with a little assistance from the sea-dragon?

Instead of preparing to go and do that which the word of the LORD commanded, Jonah decided to travel a different path. Certain voices were guiding him to go and flee another way, which he did. By now Leviathan's power of pride had taken a firm hold on the man GOD wanted to use, but where would these external influences ultimately take him?

Jonah secretly bought a ticket and boarded a ship. That particular vessel did not sail to Nineveh though. The ship Jonah was aboard had a destination course to Tarshish. Evidently the crown prince's influence successfully led the man to flee from GOD'S will, but where would he be running to?

While the ship sailed toward its objective Jonah

quickly found himself a secluded place on the vessel to hold up. He tried to be as discrete a passenger as possible and eventually fell asleep. Although this man thought he could run and hide from the heavenly assignment, the Almighty and Leviathan both knew his exact location.

A great stirring was initiated in the atmosphere around the ship. Winds began to blow and howl as the waves grew violent. From nowhere a massive storm began to rage at sea. The storm grew to such a magnitude that many aboard the tossed vessel felt doomed.

Voices started breaking out everywhere. People began speaking in different tongues and languages. Many shouted prayers to their own personal gods. And although there were various differences between those sailing together, they all had one thing in common. Everyone on the vessel contributed to do anything possible in order to survive such a horrendous onslaught at sea.

Then it finally became exposed. Through a turn of events everyone had been made aware of Jonah and him running from the GOD of Israel. Those aboard prayed and yelled that much more, screaming for the GOD of the Jews to have mercy upon them.

These men even tried to row their ship to land, but with no avail. GOD was resisting them, as the winds and the waves held this ship in the palms of its hands. Leviathan stood by with glee, watching and waiting to see what the Almighty would do with those human beings.

Then unexpectedly the crown prince experienced a bit of a surprise. Instead of the ship being wiped out and sunk by the hands of GOD, a miracle seemed to happen. It was a miracle indeed.

Although still consumed with pride Jonah did something Leviathan had not foreseen. This man gave the solution to the problem everyone faced. These people must indeed throw him overboard.

At first the men did not want to toss him off the ship. The general concern had been for everyone to be safe. Finally though Jonah's plan won many over, so he was eventually cast into the stormy sea.

Suddenly the waters and wind calmed. Almost immediately all those aboard the vessel began praising the GOD of the Jews. Everyone felt so relieved, for their lives were spared. Evidently all had been spared but one.

Jonah's body remained unseen by any. All on board thought without a doubt that this running man had become lost to the deep. Outwardly these people continued to praise GOD for HIS goodness, but some may have felt a little sadness within for the loss of Jonah.

Neither was Leviathan entirely pleased with the turn of events. He desired to see all aboard that ship sink, and wanted to claim each one of their souls. Now the Archon would just have to be satisfied with the one he thought had been obtained.

Prematurely the crown prince puffed-up in the thought of him somehow being able to alter GOD'S will. The sea-dragon believed the city of Nineveh still lingered safely in his clutches. However, the celebration became short lived.

GOD still remained in control and was about to demonstrate to the crown prince HIS majesty. With one command a large fish received orders to go and gather the body of HIS servant Jonah. The fish obeyed its call without hesitation and proceeded to swallow this physical man in one piece.

Jonah's body most likely lay there lifeless inside the fish for what may have appeared like an eternity. This occurrence had been such an ordeal that the only thing probably keeping Jonah hanging on was GOD'S mercy upon him. How had it gotten to the point where a man's body lay in a cold being from the deep while his soul seemingly lay in Sheol (or hell)?

Crying out to GOD from beyond and in the depths, the LORD heard Jonah's plea. Once again mercy came into play. GOD had compassion upon Jonah and planned to resurrect him back into the land of the living.

Commandments were quickly issued for Jonah to be restored in order to continue his mission. The sea creature that held this servant of GOD obeyed the Creator and surfaced from the depths. Per the instructions, the great fish vomited up the man onto dry land in one piece.

Jonah gasped as he took into his lungs one fresh breath after another. He was again alive and walking the surface of the earth. Without question, that one man (who after experiencing such a supernatural recovery over death itself) appeared back on track once more. Now Jonah let GOD lead, and followed along with the higher plan of getting this important job done.

Jonah finally made it to Nineveh. Right away he began to declare the word of the LORD, calling for all those in the city to repent. His words flowed with an anointing from above and began to pierce the hearts and minds of everyone.

A move of GOD could be felt throughout the city. Even the king of Nineveh called for a fast and proclaimed all should heed the words of this prophetic man. Repent, repent, repent, were the words echoed throughout the streets. And repent is what the city did.

As the people turned from their wicked ways, GOD moved. HE forgave them of their wickedness and began to restore what the watery crown prince had previously controlled and taken.

Leviathan lost his deadly grip on the city. His advantage over the inhabitants had been taken away, because people were now willingly humbling themselves before GOD and turning from their prideful attitudes.

Many were saved and their lives spared. The large metropolis was delivered from GOD'S wrath. People had been set free from Leviathan and his minions control. But what about Jonah's life? What happened to the man who brought the good news of salvation?

Jonah apparently turned loose of some of his past mistakes and failures. He would even turn loose of past experiences. Could it be that it was too hard for him to turn loose of pride?

Almost 120,000 people were saved and spared from GOD'S judgment. These same people had been freed from the bondage's which held them in the dark kingdom. They received that freedom from hearing the words Jonah spoke.

Even with so much success abounding the prophet still hated what GOD accomplished. Jonah despised the event to the degree that he did not want to physically live anymore.

The man experienced so much anguish because of GOD'S goodness toward these people of Nineveh. Easily this can be confirmed in the book of Jonah 4:3.

> "Therefore now, O LORD, take, I beseech thee, my life from me; for it is better for me to die than to live."

The information in that one verse can pose many questions. What made it possible for a man duly empowered by GOD to help bring so many people to salvation suffer himself because of the crown prince of the deep? How could a man lose sight of his own life and not care about living anymore just because he helped others find their lives? Was this extreme ideology Jonah experienced some type of retaliation from Leviathan, or could pride be so strong and powerful that a person would rather perish than live without it?

Believe Us... And The Movement

Leviathan exhibits unique authorities and vast overwhelming strengths which can easily affect those on land as well as at sea. In either case, it is still the same as plotting a course to sail from one direction to another. Whether by land or by sea, the crown prince has a destination in mind for every human being possible. His manipulative goal is to ultimately lead any man, woman, or child possible into a life of service for the sea-dragon and the dark kingdom.

To give a demonstration of how subtle the Archon can maneuver someone's life into the bonds of servitude, a short metaphorical story is told. Although the characters in the story are fictional, the example of how the crown prince operates is factual.

The story will begin with a birth of a human male

child. The new and precious little baby boy would straightway carry the name Dale Roger Caswell.

Little Dale began to experience certain problems right from the beginning of his life. There had been some physical issues. Due to those issues the young child's overall health was not good at all.

Because of the conditional concerns both his parents always kept an observant eye on their son. These two people alertly watched over the little lad as a chicken protecting her young. However, they were not the only one looking at young Dale Roger attentively. Leviathan watched everything from a distance, and waited in the shadows for the right opportunity to make his move.

Regardless of poor health issues the little boy continued to grow into manhood. While traveling through life he always found it thrilling and exciting to learn, or excel, in knowledge. It was for this one single desire that the young man boldly set out on a mission to obtain as many educational degrees possible.

Coming from a family with limited resources, Dale Roger could only work hard and hope for a good break. Eventually the young man received a surprising opportunity when a scholarship from nowhere was offered to him. Although the University promised to issue him the full ride, time would ultimately tell where this unbeknown gesture really came from.

Dale gathered some belongings and departed for the opportunity of higher learning. A new excitement could be felt all around him. For unknown reasons there seemed to be a different passion and drive in his steps now as the future appeared brighter and brighter. Little had it been realized that this human was being led onto a path taking him further into the grasp of Leviathan.

While away at school Dale became introduced to the topic of religion. He became very drawn to that particular subject and eventually decided to make it a continual part of his life.

Because these unforeseen desires were strong Dale thought it better for him to change his major. That was what he did.

After the abrupt transfer he overtly adapted quite well to the new schedule. Proceeding with his studies Dale continued to receive high marks.

Seasons flew by. Then finally the day had arrived. Before he knew it the man graduated.

After graduation it became time to apply the education toward serving as an intern. Dale felt a need to prove he had what it would take to excel in his new career. As a deep drawing within him desired advancement, the Archon rejoiced and wanted him to advance as well.

With the clock marching on this man joined the clergy. While serving in various roles Dale met a wonderful lady and married. Although he willingly took the hand of a lovely woman, hidden away was a dreadful secret he dare not share with anyone.

Apparently the man held on to a strong ideology that it was possible to live any way he wanted to or desired to, no matter what the *Bible* he spoke from said. Dale became easily convinced (by the crown prince) he should be at the center of his life, and not a GOD nor faith he swore to serve.

However, the twisted radicalism throughout the man's thoughts did not cease there. Leviathan continued to encourage him with the belief that if Dale could live self-willed to do what he pleased, why wouldn't he want to help others realize and obtain those same freedoms for themselves as well.

Years passed as Dale had become many things, like a dad and a deacon. GOD blessed the man with three wonderful kids and a wife who loved him. While the family and career began to further grow, so grew the festering ideas and concepts planted by the sea-dragon within this husband and father.

The wearing away of any morality over time caused Dale to embrace more thoughts from the dark kingdom. By now he had been mentally sold a convincing so-called truth regarding his own personal inner being. Desires were manifesting to live out what was becoming real to him. Without any hesitation there became no option for him but to live an alternate lifestyle, no matter who it may wound or betray.

Because of those choices Deacon Caswell decided to divorce his wife. Right away the process of transforming into another life began.

Not long after Dale committed to himself that he would embrace an alternative lifestyle, the Archon positioned another like-minded individual to come across the man's path. When Matt entered into the picture Leviathan gained an invested interest in two people instead of just the wayward deacon. A plan continued to form.

Dale and Matt quickly connected and soon became more than occasional lovers. Right out of nowhere these two men, who barely knew one another, moved in together and eventually became a couple.

Enhanced by their relationship the deacon became consumed with his openness of being homosexual, deliberately living a lifestyle fashioned after that which personally meant everything to him. As this public exhibition became a controversial topic within the church structure itself, Dale did little to realize that Leviathan purposely laid all these traps and snares which brought him to where he traveled today.

Meanwhile, the kingdom of darkness progressed and labored intently without ceasing in order to continue with their agenda. Conveniently an office in the church had opened up and now the plan could be furthered. Somehow Dale, a seemingly unpopular deacon with a blatant alternative lifestyle, received the opportunity for a possible advancement to become the diocese bishop.

Although there were many negative emotions generated regarding the candidate for office, surprisingly a sizeable amount of voices shouted in support for him. The crown prince and others made sure Deacon Caswell would have all the reinforcements he needed.

Any opposition quickly met with resistance, as people everywhere had an opinion of whether to challenge or approve the choice of Deacon Caswell's nomination. Regardless of his own personal lifestyle choices, this man would apparently be held up by many. However, did the actual fate and decision of the promotion really lay in human hands?

Curiously, questions circulated. Were there enough yes votes for Caswell to secure the office and become a bishop? There would most certainly be enough if Leviathan had anything to do with it.

Everyone who needed to cast a ballot did. The votes were tallied and the count very close. Caswell, along with his controversial message, received a narrow acceptance into the order and was given the position of bishop.

All of the crown prince's effort and mesmerizing

techniques worked. Through a variety of influences Caswell was off to be a leader among people. But how, and where, would the man lead? Questionably, who could be leading Bishop Caswell?

Because the election in the diocese seemed so close some celebrated the decision while others gritted their teeth. To a vast population of the people this new way of thinking became a line they were not willing to cross. To others, the act and acceptance of something so controversial and anti-scriptural was unacceptable.

Quickly a movement spread throughout the church. One decision had made the entire church body split. People who once were in unison and of like minds now chose to break coven with one another. The sea-dragon dealt a severe blow to the denomination, but he was not through by any means.

The crown prince continued to use Bishop Caswell's fame for many purposes. This person's situation was going to be the poster child for a cleaver campaign Leviathan had planned. Within one fatal swoop of vain pride, accompanied by a sideshow belief that was sold with fun-house smoke and mirrors, the kingdom of darkness gained complete authority over a multitude of people.

Bishop Caswell continued to stay busy peddling those beliefs and ideologies the sea-dragon had laid on his heart. No longer was it Dale Roger, the human being, who controlled his physical shell. The crown prince of the depths now called all the shots. It was almost like seeing a puppet on a string.

Without any hesitations the bishop continued to be called upon to exercise his popularity and proclaim the message, a message to assist the many other agendas the kingdom of darkness would put forth. And as a physical man unapologetically preached pride and disdain toward the order of a Holy GOD, the minds and ears of many listening were under assault. The objective of the onslaught was to fill every mind, and every ear, with a presence of Leviathan.

Poisons systematically spewed from the pulpit and podium as this mouthpiece for the Archon and the kingdom of darkness spoke words to confuse, alter, and ensnare the lives and souls of all. Needless to say, the spirit of Leviathan was effectively given a voice by working through those he would raise to a position of power by his might and abilities.

Allurement

The date is June 10, 1952. Today happens to be a very special day in the lives of two specific people. Somewhere in the great state of Florida, Mr. and Mrs. Frost have just received a wonderful gift from GOD. This couple has experienced the birth of their second son, Jack.

As time marched on for the Frost family everyone continued to remain in an active lifestyle. Mr. Frost held a diligent commitment to his job at the U.S. Postal Service and stayed very busy. In addition to a long work schedule he also owned a side business and managed to successfully teach tennis. His wife, Mrs. Frost, undertook the important position of a teacher.

Jack grew and grew. He went from baby to boy. Life became rich with one learning experience after another for the newly developing individual.

Around the age of eight this little boy began to realize that some things in his life did not seem quite right. It became almost impossible not to notice how his dad always treated him harshly and sternly. Through all the brashness, unbeknown to the young one, some of Leviathan's initiatives were in operation from positions already placed somewhere deep within a grown man's soul.

Jack learned early on he must strive very hard if trying to obtain an acknowledgement from his dad, because any recognition must be earned. How sad it was because the lad desperately yearned after this parents' affection. It had even gotten to the point where the little boy would be willing to attempt anything in order to hopefully gain the grown-up's approval.

Jack's dad, however, not only acted harshly and brutish with his son. Seemingly the man came across tough with most everyone. Apparently through the eyes of Mr. Frost you either had to be the best of the best or you were nothing. No handshakes or congratulations for second place. Simultaneously as the crown prince continued to overshadow and influence certain aspects of Mr. Frost's attitude and behavior, he began to further infiltrate more of the environment and mentality around Jack.

Hitting, throwing, catching, or playing any kind of game with a ball came to be something Jack had no interest in personally. Although for a season the boy did make an effort to work very hard at becoming good at the game of tennis. He committed to try thinking these actions may make his dad proud. Nevertheless, every time he missed the ball or showed any type of weakness with the game Mr. Frost let him have it unmercifully.

By the time Jack turned twelve he had become very discouraged, and grew weary in any attempt to seek his Father's approval. Jack's dad had become tougher on him than ever before. The strain between the two escalated like it had never been. In such a challenging season the Archon took any opportunity to further drive a wedge between father and son.

During the age of twelve the crown prince made another strategic move against Jack. Agents of Leviathan were assigned to bait the boy through the power of addictions and allurement. At that time, the young man became targeted for the first of many addictions.

Wisely the sea-dragon wanted to leverage addictive spirits as powerful and effective weapons against the inexperienced human, because the lad had become so desperate to find something that would smother the turmoil and pain within his very soul. But what would be the best bait to use in order to catch the mind and thoughts of a twelve-year-old human male?

In most cases, unbridled with hormones flourishing, a male of that age group would probably have curiosities in regard to a female. Questions of their own personal being could arise from these curiosities, wondering how to interact with those of the opposite sex. With that concept in mind, spirits of the water would have to do a little outsourcing to effectively accomplish this goal quickly for the kingdom of darkness.

After an approval and royal decree from the boss, certain spirits received permission for a joint operation with another governing realm in darkness. Right away minions of darkness from that realm were dispatched to comply with the overall objective to attack Jack.

Cleverly this crown prince took advantage of a weakened, emotionally tired lad and had him placed onto a path of addiction, a path which would start by initially entering into the deadly realm of pornography.

Temporarily in conjunction with another crown prince of hell for that phase of the plan, the sea-dragon did not mind using any source at his disposal to continue weakening and guiding young Jack Frost for his purpose.

Life continued to spiral further and further down for the young man. Feeling more distant from his family, while simultaneously running from an abusive father, Jack willingly accepted another addiction as a coping mechanism by the age of seventeen. Along with a strong obsession to pornography Jack began to drink alcohol whenever possible. By compounding the false comforts of alcohol with viewing pornography, Jack felt he had learned how to escape, if even for a moment, the reality of so much trauma and confusion in his life.

Although effective in their sinister endeavors, Leviathan and the kingdom of darkness weren't through with the mortal man yet. By the age of eighteen Jack's addiction to pornography and alcohol was joined by an introduction to drugs. Within no time the teenager's social drug use turned into another addiction.

All of a sudden Jack found himself bound by a three-cord strand of addictions which continuously fed off one another. It had become obvious by now this young man willingly consumed whatever would take away the pain, even if it only lasted temporarily. Through a desperate need to escape, masking the pain of Jack's reality became everything to him.

In 1972, Jack reached the age of nineteen. That was the same year he found himself confined to a hospital. Jack had been placed there because of a serious drug overdose. The drug he overdosed on was LSD, or commonly known on the streets as acid or trip.

Then in his twenties Jack became a commercial

fisherman. However, he was not just a typical deckhand. The man held a title of captain, and governed a forty-four-foot fishing boat.

The job of fishing at sea seemed appealing to Jack. This profession had become another escape from his personal life on land. Cleverly while he gravitated closer and closer to the longing of the sea, Leviathan navigated closer and closer to the unsuspecting man.

Like any other business there were always people competing. In the fishing industry, any contest began at sea with the catch. When the workday ended the competition always transferred back to the fish houses on shore or where the caught fish were to be sold.

A recorded chart was posted in many of the establishments where the commercial fishermen sold their haul. These charts kept account of the different ships and their efforts for the day, week, and possibly month. Listed there for all to see were the size and weights of everyone's catch. Whoever caught the most, and whoever caught the biggest, received the title of "top hook."

Jack became convinced by the Archon that "top hook" was a coveted title he must personally carry. Misleading ideas kept systematically promising the man if he were to walk around and be known as "top hook," it would gain him the gratification his soul so richly deserved. Additional ideas were interjected that not only could the title and prestige be satisfying to Captain Jack, but also be pleasing to his father, a man who only focused on the best and most successful.

Assisted by these influential thoughts (from the crown prince) swirling around in his mind, a choice was made. Jack decided he would be willing to do anything, or sacrifice whatever, in order to obtain this title and glory.

Whatever must be paid will be paid, all for the praise. It did not matter to him what had to happen or who he had to step on, Jack Frost was going to be "top hook" or someone would pay.

Within that constrained perimeter of unflinching attitude was how it must be, hard as nails and cold as ice. Eventually the Captain gained from those around him the nickname Captain Bligh.

Speeding forward to the winter of 1979, Captain Jack and his crew were anchored off the coast of the Carolinas. One night, over the radio, these men heard the cries of other vessels larger than theirs some miles away.

Certain ships are experiencing serious trouble because of a large storm. One ship has almost sunk while another sinks. It would seem on this night that agents from the deep roamed around churning the raging seas.

Captain Jack and his crew attentively listen to the radio while trying to ride out the storm for themselves. Ears became glued to the radio, hoping to hear any news of the Coast Guard in route to aid those hopeless souls who were about to perish. No word ever came of any help and it was eventually realized the icy waters claimed yet other victims. However, the perilous story does not end there.

Just before sunrise a big wave slammed into Captain Jack's fishing vessel. This surge hit the side so hard that the force of the impact snapped the anchor line and set the boat adrift.

Immediately another large wave followed and struck the unstable boat. That wave hit the floundering vessel and turned it sideways. Now it would seem as if Jack and his whole crew were to suffer the same tragic fate as others had before them in the storm. Were these men to be forever lost to the murky depths?

Suddenly for those on the boat this world seemed to be coming to an end. Their lives probably flashed before their eyes. Then in a split moment of time, without showing any reservation, Captain Jack cried out saying "God save me."

There would be no way to describe what took place next but a miracle. Somehow the small fishing boat swayed back and seemingly corrected itself after Jack cried out to GOD. The men and their sea vessel were saved and had survived a storm which earlier sank larger ships and taken other lives.

The mercy of GOD delivered these sailors from the sea. HIS goodness had overshadowed their situation and spared the lives of Captain Jack, his crew, and ship. Things could have turned out differently though for those men who were placed in such a dangerous and unpredictable situation.

What could be said today of this particular story if Captain Jack Frost had not called out to GOD and asked to be saved from the sea? What may have happened if the Captain just quit and gave in to the face of adversity? Where would these men have ended up if Captain Jack willingly surrendered to the perilous situation, the deep blue sea, and the ultimate will of the crown prince Leviathan.

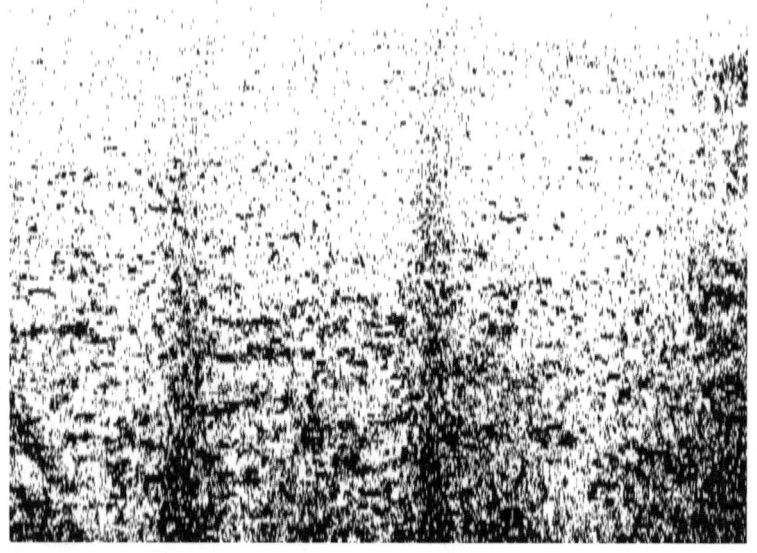

Chapter 5

Other Names and Faces of Leviathan

Leviathan existed long before humanities creation on the planet. Having been encased within an icy prison here in this world by GOD, then set free to roam for a season, the Archon continues to lead a charge to undo GOD'S ordained representation on earth: mankind.

Because of his lengthy existence, there should be no doubt that the human race was diligently studied by the alien from the beginning of Adam and Eve. Through these extensive observations the crown prince has cleverly learned a variety of tactics in the art of how to manipulate his personal persona and idealogies to many.

To reiterate one such example of the fore-mentioned premise take the first chapter. Alluded to in the beginning of that chapter, when Leviathan is mentioned in the public arena a majority of people naturally think of a whale or big oceanic animal, and rightfully so. That particular idea has been taught and written in all but a few dictionaries or points of reference.

There is however more to the sea-dragon than commonly known in average everyday society. Realistically, from an early age of time the spirit of Leviathan has received countless acknowledgements through numerous names, identities, ideas, and movements.

In a unique comparison the same idea could reflect how a lot of human beings are acknowledged in today's world. Many people are usually known by a first, middle, and last name. Added to that particular principle can be other types of names like nicknames, surnames, or what may be called reflective names. While these practices apply to a person, the same ideology is applicable to Leviathan as well.

With a basic explanation given expressing the concept of name variations, it is time to initiate an exploration into other avenues the crown prince has leveraged for himself. Before beginning to explore these various ways of the sea-dragon, a caution and warning must be issued.

In this particular chapter, certain information of an occult nature will be presented. The applicable information will be kept to the topic at hand and given only as evidence to the validity of the topic. These points are not presented to promote the reading of, or exploration into any occultism.

Occultism is full of dangerous and deadly ideologies promoting the dark kingdom. These practices have been set forth for one thing, and that would be to ensnare every human soul possible somewhere within the realms of hell.

It is recommended that if there are any occult items, books, or propaganda in your home, it would be properly disposed of as soon as possible. The reason behind this action is simply because every occult item constructed has had a demonic spirit assigned to that particular object, book, movie, or other. So by allowing that item in your home, a demon has been allowed there as well.

An Entity of the Sea

Leviathan through a vast agenda has openly received admiration and worship from many human beings throughout time. Willingly, or with unknown comprehension, various creeds and cultures have consented their efforts to give the crown prince vast amounts of adoration.

One example can be taken from the mainline ideologies promoted within ancient Greek mythology. Contained in these legends there were gods for this and gods for that.

To give a quick overview in accordance to the doctrine, a list of entities apparently formed from Chaos (or nothingness). Those beings would come to be known as primordial gods. As the understanding continues these primordial gods begin to form the heavens and earth.

There seems to be, however, evidence not only contradicting that information, but proving the actual validity of such an idea as truly false and misleading. The Creator of the universe stated facts contrary to what this mythology presents. Recorded in *The Holy Bible's* Old Testament book of Genesis 1:1 is GOD'S given account of creation.

> "In the beginning God created the heaven and the earth."

It is clear there was one GOD, and not a large group of gods that initiated the beginning and creation. Without question it was ordained by the hand of the Almighty, and not multiple entities, of how to place, mold, and shape the earth and the cosmos.

Leviathan would never allow something like truth to stand in the way of his objective to deceive, mislead, and ensnare humanity. The crown prince will instigate and support any believable tale just to lift himself up in the eyes of his sworn enemy: mankind.

To continue an examination into certain portions of Greek mythology, there were primordial deities comprised of male and female characteristics. These easily represent different aspects of the crown prince. None stand out like the Greek sea god Pontus.

According to legend Pontus was supposedly the beginning, or king, over the depths of the sea at creation. He became first to rule over the seas, followed by the reign of his brother Oceanus. After Oceanus the next ruler of the deep would apparently be the famous Poseidon.

Reportedly the strength and energy of Pontus seemed as the tossing and churning of the ocean waves. His depiction before people likened to that of a large human head emerging from water. On his head were two horns in the shape of crab claws.

Continuing with the myth Pontus brought about many offspring. These children were manifested as water deities. Some fables even go further to suggest through Pontus all sea life came about.

Another portion of this belief can be quickly challenged. GOD shared in HIS *Word* the truth of who brought about the earth's seas, and how the oceanic inhabitance came into existance. Taken from the book of Genesis, the actual accounts pertaining to those segments of creation can be seen.

The evidence provided is taken from two different places in chapter 1 of Genesis. The first reference are verses 9-10.

> 9. And God said, Let the waters under the heaven be gathered together unto one place, and let the dry land appear: and it was so.
>
> 10. And God called the dry land Earth; and the gathering together of the waters called he Seas: and God saw that it was good.

There are two interesting points to highlight from this example. First, it can be clearly seen where GOD instructed *"the waters under the heaven be gathered together"* and situated.

The second point is our Creator chose to name the gathered waters seas and decided *"it was good."* Could it be that because GOD thought the seas were a *"good"* thing reason enough for Leviathan to attempt to deceive humans into thinking the seas were his creation?

As previously mentioned, there would be a second reference to aid in unraveling this deceptive mythological doctrine. That reference will come from Genesis 1:20-22.

> 20. And God said, Let the waters bring forth abundantly the moving creature that hath life, and fowl that may fly above the earth in the open firmament of heaven.
>
> 21. And God created great whales, and every living creature that moveth, which the waters brought forth abundantly, after their kind, and every winged fowl after his kind: and God saw that it was good.

> 22. And God blessed them, saying, Be fruitful, and multiply, and fill the waters in the seas, and let fowl multiply in the earth.

Without question these verses not only prove GOD created the seas, but explain where the Almighty made those that dwell within the seas. Printed are words which clearly show where HE made *"great whales, and every living creature that moveth"* in water.

Verse 22 can plainly confirm where *"God blessed them, saying, Be fruitful, and multiply, and fill the waters in the seas,"* by HIS decree. Undeniably it was the Almighty who created and blessed the production and reproduction of all those who dwell in water.

GOD chose to bring about life in the deep. Watery beings were never created because of the will of some entity named Pontus, nor were they fashioned by a false deity like the sea-dragon.

His and Hers

In one collection of old writings, Leviathan's indoctrination has been craftily maneuvered into receiving a multitude of acknowledgements and vast glorification through an ideology of duel deities; combining a god and goddess of water and sea. Dating back to ancient Babylon, the Archon disguised himself among a mythological aspect as both the masculine identity of Aspu (the god of fresh water) and the feminine identity of Tiamat (the goddess of the salt sea).

In a basic concept, written within the *Enuma Elish*, the first two god-heads come together and begin to blend watery creations. The beginning of that ideology will read like this.

> "When above the heavens did not yet exist nor the earth below, Apsu the freshwater ocean was there, the first, the begetter, and Tiamat, the saltwater sea, she who bore them all; they were still mixing their eaters, and no pasture land had yet been formed, nor even a reed marsh."

The legend soon states Aspu (or sometimes known as Abzu) is overthrown and slain by his own progenies. Because of the slaying of Aspu, Tiamat became enraged and plotted war on those who murdered him. She becomes chaos, and eventually Tiamat took on the embodiment of a massive sea-dragon.

As the story continues Tiamat physically suffered defeat at the hand of the god Marduk. He has taken the sea-dragon and *"smashed her skull"* with a club. The *Enuma Elish* then states Marduk *"cut through the channels of her blood,"* dividing Tiamat in half.

The story does not end with the death of Tiamat's physical being. Reportedly, from using different parts of the dragon's body Marduk then began to build portions of the heavens and earth.

In this ancient account Leviathan had been overwhelmingly glamorized from two different aspects. He effectively depicted a fabricated pretense of two deities whom united and created a new beginning from water. The crown prince covertly positioned himself in order to equally demonstrate the masculine and feminine facets of a human personality. Seemingly the Archon wanted to capitalize by attracting both male and female genders.

Cleverly constructed, the myth then attempts to relay an ideology that segments of heaven and earth were literally formed from portions of the sea-dragon. Apparently Leviathan must think so highly of himself as to be seen as the beginning substance of many things which were to be made and fashioned.

Holy Scripture openly debunks the entire account. It plainly states in the Old Testament book of Genesis 1:1 who created the universe.

> "In the beginning God created the heaven and the earth."

Most certainly the truth can be no more evident. Father GOD created the cosmos and all that is contained therein. HE was the true beginning before everything and everyone, including the Archon Leviathan.

Fish Food

Now travel back to a distant period in the past. Somewhat mysteriously altered, Leviathan's massive presence easily circulated deceptively among many of the early Canaanite people. The crown prince covertly received their praises through a deity that went by the name Yam (or Yamm).

Overall, the dynamics of this specific deity's personification portrayed a godlike image who lorded over the rivers and the seas. Due to the sole persona of the entity commonly intertwined to harshness and chaos, the

Other Names and Faces of Leviathan

name Yam carries a Semitic interpretation and connotation relating said name to the power and virility of the sea.

Canaanite mythology also presented a depiction of a heavenly war between deities. The war began, among other things, because a leader named Yam conducted himself as a tyrant over his subordinates.

As the war in that story continued Yam eventually suffered a devastating defeat. Ultimately he was struck down to earth and finally beaten. This water deity had been driven from the heavenly places because of his wickedness.

How interesting to see where another society of people have, throughout time, told of some cosmic being defeating a hardened entity from the sea. Indeed there had been a great battle fought in the heavenly realms and a ferocious sea being was defeated, but not exactly as the Canaanites of that day believed.

Although this story may have been infused with similarities of other stories from one creed or another, and from one culture or another, ultimately one fact remains the same. *GOD'S Word* is quite accurate concerning the authority HE has had and can exert over Leviathan.

Another example of this is written in the Old Testament book of Psalms 74:13-14. Here is a statement of what GOD can easily do to Leviathan.

> **13. Thou didst divide the sea by thy strength: thou breakest the heads of the dragons in the waters.**

> 14. Thou brakest the heads of leviathan in pieces, and gavest him to be meat to the people inhabiting the wilderness.

Without any confusion these verses demonstrate what GOD is able to do to the crown prince effortlessly. Here it is shown where the Almighty can *"divide the sea"* to break Leviathan apart and render him helpless before humanity. With no reservations it is clearly proclaimed who Leviathan's real master was and continues to be: the I AM.

Reflective Names: The King of Children

A presence or representation of Leviathan can be noticed by what will be called reflective names. Reflective names are titled acknowledgements someone is given or known by because of the actions, examples, positions, character, or demonstrations of their lives. In other words, it is a way to reflect who an individual is, acts like, or has become in a particular role.

There are many examples of this premise. A positive example could be a local law enforcement officer who can also be known as a first responder, a police office, a sheriff, deputy, or detective, not to mention being known by other independent ranks like sergeant or captain. The Archon is no different when relating to reflective names.

Varieties of names and other characteristics for the crown prince can be mentioned, but for time sake only a select few will be shared. Some of those terms reflect different viewpoints of who this spiritual being truly is within, while other attributes can reveal the ideologies he could manifest or bring about when near.

These applications for Leviathan are also affirmed through *Scripture*. The reflective names with *biblical* reference points to different aspects of the individual will read as follows.

Reflective Names and Characteristic References

1. King of Pride	Job 41: 34
2. Selfishness	James 3:16
	Proverbs 28:25
3. Contentious	Proverbs 13:10
4. Scorner	Proverbs 21:24
5. Haughty Spirit	Proverbs 16:18

To give a combined summation for all the names listed, the most oblivious reflective term for the crown prince would simply be king of pride. He has made it to the leadership status because of an evil ability for truly knowing how to exemplify the dark ways, and exercising those ways proficiently over others.

This information is so important that GOD made sure to declare in HIS *Word* a parallel association between the act of pride and a being called Leviathan. The seadragon's position is clearly stated and documented in the Old Testament book of Job 41:34.

> "He beholdeth all high things: he is a king over all the children of pride."

When the verse states this crown prince has *"beholdeth all high things"* it can simply be giving a reference determining Leviathan has seen and witnessed great and small events throughout many spiritual and physical realms. The verse further ensures the reader that as the Archon has beheld *"high things"* from time past, he still *"beholdeth"* situations, circumstances, and *"all high"* and lofty things of today.

Placed also within the verse are ideas of who are in fact subjects, or *"children"* of a *"king"* in darkness. Could he actually be governing multitudes of people who walk, live, and dedicate themselves to an ungodly pursuance of a prideful lifestyle? Are these kinds of individuals either unknowingly, or knowingly, submitting themselves to the will of an invisible leader named Leviathan?

Defeated

Although the Archon is an extremely powerful soldier in the kingdom of darkness, he is not completely invincible. Not many people can claim to have faced this giant alone and walked away from the encounter unscathed.

These words should not discourage anyone though. There is good news. It is possible for any person to beat the sea-dragon.

Therefore, for anyone who would either like to possibly gain more insight regarding this alien being, or who would like to learn how a person can gain the authority needed to defeat a powerful alien like Leviathan, it can be as simple as turning the page and beginning to read chapter six, A Defeated Foe.

Chapter 6

A Defeated Foe

MANY ASPECTS OF the crown prince are yet to be covered. Regardless of any further input it would be undeniable to state that Leviathan is a very powerful entity.

Throughout these pages there have been numerous illustrations given to demonstrate his strength and might, proving this Archon wields a superior authority in the physical realm as well as the spiritual realm. Without question it can be assured the sea-dragon is a worthy foe which should never be taken lightly. Nevertheless, even with those massive abilities and dominions Leviathan will never be able to claim the title of complete invincibility.

First in the final chapter of this book are recorded times throughout history where the crown prince has undertaken humiliation and suffered defeat. Next, two previous stories will be revisited in an attempt to further expose certain aspects of Leviathan's downfall. Then finally revealed is the knowledge of how the sea-dragon can suffer defeat by anyone today.

A One - Two Punch

Initially GOD created an untainted, zealous, and powerful being named Leviathan. Since the spiritual falling away, actions have been recorded of the Creator publicly holding that Archon accountable throughout history. There should be no doubt in the capabilities of these actions from on high, because the Almighty already foreknew everything there was to know about the sea-dragon and how to defeat him.

The first documented time this fierce and almost unstoppable being experienced a major defeat at the hand of GOD began in the heavens. During the heavenly war, in the celestial city, Leviathan stood guilty for his attempt to overthrow GOD'S order. It was there in the celestial city where the Archon hung his head in defeat and shame.

The second of the one-two punch landed its blow to the crown prince some two thousand years ago. This particular punch was delivered from a place on earth called Golgotha, known then as the place of the skull. At Golgotha, the Son of GOD freely gave His life as a ransom for humanity. That place happened to be where Jesus hung on a cross, shedding His precious blood to wash away the sins of every human being who would accept and receive it.

With the one-two punch GOD gave the crown prince, HE demonstrated who still held charge over the sea-dragon. GOD showed Leviathan that every time he would be in the Almighty's presence, defeat would be a common place. What a subjected existence for one so lofty, just because he chose to rebel against his Creator and side with Lucifer.

A Date with Defeat

Although the crown prince is active and mobile today in wielding his darkness from the depths, there is an event

A Defeated Foe

the massive entity will completely yield for. Leviathan has a specific appointment there will be no getting out of. That particular appointment was not scheduled by the sea-dragon himself, but by GOD.

GOD openly set a specific time aside where HE will focus strictly on Leviathan, and the event has been publicly recorded. Written in *The Holy Bible's* Old Testament book of Isaiah 27:1 is an explanation of GOD'S plan for this crown prince.

> "In that day the LORD with his sore and great and strong sword shall punish leviathan the piercing serpent, even leviathan that crooked serpent; and he shall slay the dragon that is in the sea."

Plainly seen in GOD'S *Word* Leviathan's days are numbered. GOD said HE would *"punish"* Leviathan eventually. GOD also stated HE will *"slay the dragon that is in the sea."* Undeniably what GOD said HE would do HE will do. Leviathan may try to run or hide from the Almighty, but he cannot escape the living GOD.

Collectively, without any misinterpretations it can be accurately stated the Almighty defeated Leviathan in the heavens and at Golgotha. Also evident through the reading of *The Holy Scriptures*, Leviathan has another date with defeat at the hand of GOD. Obviously, without reserve our Creator openly demonstrated once again that HE is greater than the Archon could ever be.

Multitudes of questions remain. Questions such as where does mankind actually stand in regard to the crown prince? Is it realistically possible for a human being to obtain a level of power and authority great enough to defeat the mighty sea-dragon? In addition, if it were possible to gain such an ability what must an individual do in order to receive that strength to defeat Leviathan?

Regarding these three questions mentioned, there are clear answers to those wondersome thoughts. And they will be addressed. Before these questions can be answered, let's revisit two previous stories from earlier in this book.

Surviving the Movement

In the forth chapter we met Bishop Dale Roger Caswell and the alternative lifestyle movement he cleverly encouraged. In that particular story certain beliefs and ideologies were promoted relentlessly, and simultaneously used to bring confusion in an attempt to unravel GOD'S divine order.

Over the years, many people who heard Bishop Caswell's sermons and took them to heart became disillusioned, misguided, or confused. Mind-altering spirits from Leviathan had been set free to bring harm every time this man spoke to the public. One such person listening in the vast audiences happened to be a young man named Larry.

Larry was twenty-two when he first heard a sermon from Bishop Caswell. He heard those very eloquently presented words because the bishop received an invitation to be a guest speaker at Larry's church. While the spiritual leader's demeanor seemed nonthreatening at that time, his words were directed to pierce the souls of those who heard them.

A Defeated Foe

When the bishop blatantly and openly condoned an alternate sexual lifestyle from behind the pulpit of Larry's church, a good number of those in attendance were taken by surprise. Some repelled at his sermon while others disregarded the man's words as rants and raves. Still to others in the congregation, the bishop demonstrated a more modern philosophy and seemed to be up with the times. Then there were those who became confused and began to ponder within their own thoughts. Larry happened to be one of those people.

Another reason for Larry's growing confusion had been because Leviathan was already effectively at work in his life. Prior to the surprising message, minions of the crown prince had used attack after attack to weaken Larry in many areas. Successfully the plan started to have its effects and began throwing this unsuspecting young man off balance.

One major impact had recently taken place which appeared to sideswipe his new marriage. Through many influences of prideful relatives and high-minded friends, his wife of one year chose to leave Larry and filed for a divorce. Effectively the workings of the sea-dragon continued to convince her that she was better than Larry, so much so, until the time had come to move on.

Left alone and abandoned by his spouse for no other reason than meddling from the crown prince, Larry could not understand why these things were happening. Ultimately he felt betrayed by a woman who said she would love him for better or worse forever.

At those vulnerable moments agents from the Archon began to whisper numerous words into the man's ears. "See, you can't trust a woman" reverberating with "all women will abandon you and mistreat you like this" were the ideas attempting to fill his thoughts. Then day after day, sometimes even hour after hour, these servants of the deep kept their relentless bombardments to infiltrate Larry's mind.

As if things were not challenging enough, now there was a religious leader who publicly and openly condoned the concept of same sex romantic relationships. With this new perspective being interjected, in addition to the words Leviathan had preached earlier, the two ideologies quickly attached themselves in support against the human.

Motivated by the language he heard from such a seemingly holy man as Bishop Caswell, Larry decided to give an alternative lifestyle some thought and consideration.

Soon after those decisions were made of presenting an openness to the bait that had been offered, Larry eventually became persuaded and convinced of his homosexual tendencies. In light of an apparent new reality some things had to change, and they had to change quick.

One of the first suggestions to aid the process of coming out publicly was to get enrolled with a gay dating site. Motivated through crafty encouragement from spirits of Leviathan, Larry put out a profile to intermingle right away with other registered members.

Almost instantaneously the young man began receiving email after email. One male after another wanted to meet him for romance. All of a sudden the whole scenario seemed quite odd and made Larry very uncomfortable.

Seemingly overtaken by these strange and unnatural experiences Larry began to rethink his choice. However, the pause only lasted momentarily. The sea-dragon

A Defeated Foe

stood ready to make a move in order to hook this human and reel him in.

With no time to waste, Larry became guided with a proposal to not view this new way of life through the eyes of romance yet. From nowhere a suggestively imposed thought shouted the idea that maybe what he needed first was a good friend who lived the alternate lifestyle.

A cleaver ideology and strategy began to take hold of something within the man's thought process. After all, a good friend is what he really sought after. While he kept willingly taking the bait Larry's preparation continued in order to be eventually led to someone specifically designed by Leviathan.

While Larry's actions began to heavily gravitate toward a lifestyle so contrary to GOD'S order, something else began to happen simultaneously. There were movements occurring which the Archon had not yet seen.

Larry's mom and sister noticed him changing certain things in his life. They gave him ample space but still tried to be there for Larry as much as he would allow them to be. These two people knew the divorce had been tough on him, not realizing how hard it really was. With keeping private the young man never let his loved ones know that life had begun to take its toll.

Surprising news surfaced when Larry told his mother and sister he now considered himself a homosexual. When the two heard the shocking statement they did not know how to respond or what to do. Finding out such a drastic change already took place within such a small amount of time was overwhelming. In no way had anyone ever thought this guy would turn gay, because it had never been in his nature at all.

One day Larry's mom mentioned to Dean, one of her

neighbor's, what the young man was going through. She did not share that kind of information with everyone but felt she could with her neighbor because something seemed different about him. He always acted kind, sincere, and professed to be a Christian.

Without any hesitation Dean told his neighbor he would gladly pass her son's name on to his church for prayer. Dean did just that. Larry's name had now been placed on a list of people who were prayed for.

However, Dean's church was not just a building where certain people gathered a few times a week. That particular church thrived to be a place where the presence of GOD could be felt. These people who assembled here loved Jesus, served GOD, and moved by HIS Spirit.

Those prayer warriors earnestly lifted up Larry and his situation. They continued to intercede and asked GOD to intervene in this circumstance. And HE did.

GOD began to move upon Larry. Not long after the prayers went up the wayward man began to feel convicted about certain lifestyle choices. Apparently wherever he went Larry could never shake those feelings.

One day he happened to be at his mother's house. They were in the yard when Dean arrived home from work. She quickly brought the young man next door for a personal introduction.

Dean and Larry shook hands and exchanged greetings. The three chatted for a moment or two. As their brief conversation began to end he invited Larry to church.

A strange silence took place for a few seconds. "Thanks for the invitation, but I already attend a church that adhere's to Bishop Caswell's teachings," Larry replies.

"I've heard of Bishop Caswell and the message he

preaches," Dean responded. "But if you ever change your mind, the invitation is still open."

Nevertheless, GOD'S Holy Spirit urged Dean on. "Larry, let me tell you a short story about a man named Jesus, and what He preached when here on earth."

At first Leviathan tried to stop Larry from hearing the truth, but the hand of GOD momentarily subdued the sea-dragon's strength. GOD opened up Larry's ears and heart right there on his mom's lawn, and anointed the words HE gave Dean to speak into this misguided young man's life.

Larry began to hear and receive the truth. The power of the Almighty started to shatter any darkness Leviathan and Bishop Caswell cleverly placed over this person's mind, will, and emotions. Finally Larry knew the truth, and accepted what GOD was willing to give him through Jesus Christ: eternal life.

Right there on the lawn in front of witnesses Larry gave his heart to GOD and dedicated his life to Jesus. With everything the man gained right there in that moment of conversion, he gained the power to defeat Leviathan.

Reeling in Another Catch at Sea

Let's revisit another story from chapter four of this book and catch up to its continual progression. One segment told a story of addictions, unhealthy allurements, and the effects certain enticements had on an individual named Jack Frost.

The year was 1979. Captain Jack Frost, his men, and ship have been saved from a violent storm which took many larger ships, along with their crews, to the bottom abyss.

These men on one single vessel, however, were saved because the Captain acted. That man became motivated enough to suppress the stronghold of his pride, if but for a moment, and called out to a living GOD for mercy.

The Creator heard these words and moved in a seemingly hopeless situation. None would be lost, as the hand of the Almighty kept Jack and those with him safe throughout the storm.

What a supernatural occurrence. Human lives miraculously were spared from the depths. Jack and his crew received the chance to go home once again from the sea.

Regardless of the miraculous display of mercy and grace, this Captain did not completely surrender to the will of the Most High. Out of all that happened it seemed Jack's moment to call upon GOD'S presence had been genuine at the time of need, yet would it last?

Time marched on. It is now February 1980.

Even with the miracle of his existence being spared months earlier, the Captain's life still continued to function in disarray. The brutality, anger, and numerous addictions had no intention of vanishing, simply because these particular beliefs were ingrained deep in the man's soul. From a young age Jack had been conditioned mentally and emotionally and it became the only way he knew how to live and survive.

Yearning from within for something greater than he had always known, Jack decided it might be wise to separate himself from others. So back to the high seas it was as the Captain plotted a new course and set sail.

When he traveled far enough away to suit himself, he sat there with nothing around but water and sky. With an

A Defeated Foe

overwhelming desperation churning within this man's very soul Jack began to seek GOD and call out to the Creator of the universe. Without any doubt the Captain had to know if there was a GOD, and if this supernatural being really heard him.

Jack remained at sea for three days seeking some type of sign or answer from above. While the man earnestly sought after GOD, he genuinely desired to receive some divine impartations from the Almighty.

Then something supernatural began to take place as Jack received a visitation from the presence of GOD. Through that divine encounter this man became instantly delivered from the toxic and unfruitful habits which had overtaken him for so many years. GOD moved as the Almighty gave Jack Frost a new heart and a new beginning at life.

However, although so many breakthroughs occurred, things were seemingly far from over. Neither GOD, nor Leviathan, had finished with Jack yet.

As the new person inside Jack tried to emerge some things did not change. The Captain who once felt passionately driven to addictions, the sea, or whatever else made him feel good, did not stop with an obsessive behavior.

Subsequently, now the obsession behavior became cloaked in other ways. Instead of running to booze or pornography he ran to church and all the religious practices that were sociably acceptable in the eyes of people.

Jack's name had been placed in GOD'S Book of Life, but even now the man found himself in a position of not freely enjoying the love of his heavenly Father. Lurking around somewhere within were still the issues of a healthy self-approval viewpoint, something attributed to by his childhood upbringing. Apparently this performance-based acceptance concept continued to be strong enough to overflow into his newly developing relationship with GOD.

These dysfunctional ideas kept resurfacing because there was still a very serious problem hidden somewhere. A problem more than likely attached to the workings of Leviathan. Obliviously, the reason those crippling ideologies continued to manifest was simply because the crown prince still loomed over vast territories within Jack's life.

Jack quickly dove right into religion and began to become extremely busy in doing things for GOD. The man's thoughts were if he had to work hard in order to gain the approval of his earthly father, why would there be any difference regarding his heavenly Father.

By 1984, certain things began to mirror his previous life. Once again Jack could gain public acclamation as he had done in the past with the acknowledgement of "top hook." However, this time he would carry the acknowledgement and title of Pastor.

Transformed publicly the Captain could now be called the Pastor. And as he had captained a crew at sea, Jack may once again experience himself taking charge and leading a group of people.

Also in commonality were the size of the vessels. When he set sail Jack's ship was not the biggest on the seas, but the command belonged to him. In like kind the church he guided on land wasn't a large church, but it did happen to be where he held the title of leader.

Jack looked forward to the religious responsibilities as they continued to increase. Eventually the demand of the position began to take a toll on him and all those at

A Defeated Foe

home. Finally it had gotten to the point where in the eyes of his family Jack seemingly traded the love of the sea for the love of religion.

Everyone in the family, including Jack, knew something had to change right away. Without any hesitations he began to seek GOD as he had done at sea in 1980. Jack had been made aware there was still more work to be done in his life.

Then in 1994, the illusions regarding the Archon's wayward ideology started to unravel. GOD began to show Jack new and wonderful things he never thought of. GOD gave Jack insightful revelations of HIS love for this man; a love that was unconditional, and cost the Almighty dearly.

A year or so later Jack and his wife were attending a healing conference. At that conference, as Jack humbled himself even further before a presence of a Holy GOD, Father moved even more upon this human being.

Tears fell from the eyes of a person who at one time had been compared to the sea pirate Captain Bligh. Swells of emotion flooded out of him as he experienced the grace and love of GOD in a unique and special way.

Now the true light had shined upon the dark depths of a wounded soul and all the lies of Leviathan exposed. GOD poured out HIS empowering and healing Spirit upon Mr. Jack Frost in order to bring restoration into his soul and life. Successfully through the effort, a wholeness transpired as the Almighty filled those void places in the man's heart.

In his book Jack wrote about the encounter he had with GOD'S Spirit in 1995. Simply entitled *Experiencing The Father's Embrace*, Jack stated "My pride had been shattered." When that final blow from GOD shattered the pride within this man's life, Leviathan's hold over him was broken forever.

On March 5th, 2007, Mr. Jack Frost physically transitioned to be with his Lord. All his service to GOD and ministry to humanity will shine on continuously.

He left on earth a loving partner and wife named Trisha, a son named Joshua, and a daughter named Sarah. Mr. Frost also left a functioning movement his wife carries on, a movement that preaches GOD'S unconditional love. This movement can be found at Shiloh Place Ministries.

How Humanity Can Defeat Leviathan

Now it is time to address those three questions asked earlier in the beginning of this chapter. The first question was where does mankind actually stand in regard to the crown prince?

The answer to that question goes like this. No person, or people, within their own strength can ultimately oppose the crown prince. When Adam and Eve bowed to the kingdom of darkness in the Garden of Eden, all human rights to legitimate governance over the earth were transferred to the dark lord and his delegates.

The second question was is it realistically possible for a human being to obtain a level of power and authority great enough to defeat the mighty sea-dragon?

Yes is the answer to that question. Any human can obtain enough power and authority to defeat Leviathan.

The final question asked if it were possible to gain such an ability, what must an individual do in order to receive that strength to defeat Leviathan?

Before beginning any explanation pertaining to that

question, one more fact must be added in. That fact would be GOD, and the love our Creator has for HIS creation.

GOD'S love and promise of salvation for humanity is proclaimed throughout many verses and passages recorded in *The Holy Scriptures*. Most *biblical* verses and passages on these topics are written literally and straight to the point. There are, however, some verses and passages which also can be seen through a metaphoric viewpoint; to paint a clearer picture for presenting the truth.

Although literal and metaphoric verses and passages are two different types of examples, both *biblical* forms will always confirm one another. In order to elaborate the differences between the two an example of each style will be given.

The first example will be metaphoric and come from the Old Testament book of Psalms. Highlighted in that particular book is a prime description of GOD demonstrating one way HE will stand with HIS people against the workings of Leviathan and his legions. This example is located in Psalms 124:2-8.

> 2. If it had not been the LORD who was on our side, when men rose up against us;
>
> 3. Then they had swallowed us up quick, when their wrath was kindled against us:
>
> 4. Then the waters had overwhelmed us, the stream had gone over our soul:
>
> 5. Then the proud waters had gone over our soul.

> 6. Blessed be the LORD, who hath not given us as a prey to their teeth.
>
> 7. Our soul is escaped as a bird out of the snare of the fowlers: the snare is broken, and we are escaped.
>
> 8. Our help is in the name of the LORD, who made heaven and earth.

What a picture that statement portrays. It can be seen in the passage where *"If it had not been the LORD who was on our side,"* or the side of HIS people, servants of Leviathan and the kingdom of darkness could easily have *"swallowed us up"* and *"overwhelmed"* many eventually.

Stated also was the fact accrediting *"the LORD, who hath not given us as a prey to their teeth."* GOD demonstrated not only a willingness to protect HIS people, but also moved in order that their enemy's *"snare is broken,"* whereby allowing many to escape the captivity of sin.

Finally, a powerful statement is issued and could sum up a majority of questions. This statement concludes that humanity's *"help is in the name of the LORD, who made heaven and earth."*

In order to demonstrate the second type of *biblical* example in revealing GOD'S love and commitment toward humanity a literal verse must be given. The verse explains what GOD willingly did, and what HE physically gave up to save mankind from eternal damnation. Made known within these words was the true cost to deliver people from the bonds of sin and break the grasp of Leviathan and his evil minions.

Those precious words are taken from the New

A Defeated Foe

Testament book of Saint John. Presented in that particular writing is a clear demonstration of the dedication GOD showed toward HIS creation. John 3:16 can sum everything up.

> "For GOD so loved the world, that he gave his only begotten Son, that whosoever believeth in him should not perish, but have everlasting life."

How mind-blowing humanly it is to see what GOD had to provide for humanity to be set free from death, and transformed through unyielding power. HE gave the precious life of GOD'S *"only begotten Son,"* so every man, woman, and child could have a chance to be redeemed from the generational curse of sin and forgiven for any transgressions which have been committed willfully or unknowingly. What an amazing gift, and what an expensive cost for peoples' eternal freedom.

Just because GOD gave such a gift as never seen before in the cosmos does not automatically activate the results of the gift into every person's life. A gift can be given, but that is only part of the transaction. A gift must also be received by the beneficiary; because if something is given, yet not accepted, then the legitimate ownership has not been transferred to the intended recipient.

Simply put it is the same method with eternal life. GOD made a way where each person can live forever in peace, harmony, and have a second chance to exist the way it was intended by our Creator from the beginning of time. Ultimately it is each person's free will and choice to choose HIS path or not.

HIS path is this. Written in the New Testament book

of John is a clear, straight to the point directive for how someone can obtain life eternal. That literal decree is located in John 6:14.

> "Jesus saith unto him, I am the way, the truth, and the life: no man cometh unto the Father, but by me."

Plainly stated in *Scripture*, there is no way to have eternal life and forgiveness of sins without Jesus. This one step, and event, is so important a sample prayer was included for anyone who would like to receive the free gift of eternal life from GOD. It is possible to obtain that gift right now, right there, if this kind of prayer is prayed with sincere commitment.

Sample Prayer

Father, in the name of Jesus, I ask You to forgive me of all my sins. I confess that I am a sinner and need Your help. Your Word says in John 3:16 that You so loved the world that You gave Your only begotten Son, Jesus, that whosoever believes in Him should not perish but have everlasting life. Right now, by my free will, I believe that Jesus died for me and shed His blood for my sins. I choose to accept what He did for me and make Jesus Lord of my life. Help me to live a life pleasing to You. Thank You for saving me. In Jesus name I pray. Amen.

If you or someone you know just prayed that prayer or a prayer like it, then you, or them, have now become a child of the Most High GOD. Congratulations on making an eternal decision for your life. Also, welcome to the

A Defeated Foe

family. May our heavenly Father bless you, keep you, and guide you along your journey with HIM through the path of life.

However, if this prayer or a prayer like it has never been prayed with sincerity and genuine acceptance, there is another path to travel. If a human life past the age of accountability expires without any forgiveness granted by GOD for the generational curse of sin and all past transgressions, that event would cause that human soul to be transported to a place never intended for mankind.

This place was created and designed for Lucifer, Leviathan, and the kingdom of darkness, not humanity. Realistically GOD does not send human beings to the dreaded place. People ultimately send themselves there by rejecting GOD'S plan and way of salvation and redemption.

To contrary belief, each person possesses the authority to send their own eternal being to heaven or damnation. That action is allowed to occur because every human being has been gifted with the ability of free will. In light of this information there must be a conscious decision to travel either GOD'S way or Leviathan's way. GOD'S way will lead to a joyous eternal life through Christ Jesus, whereas Leviathan's way will only lead to sorrow, misery, and finally eternal destruction.

These are the two paths into eternal life, and a choice must be made. But beware to those who do not want to make a decision. By not making any choice to ask GOD for forgiveness while alive, utter death would automatically be determined as a forfeiture to the kingdom of darkness if for no other reason than the afflicting generational sin curse applied to all humanity from Adam and Eve's failure.

Parting Words

Now has come the time to once again close another volume in *The Leadership Series: Heads of War*. Thank you for taking the time to read these writings.

This book was created to share an awareness, bring a preparedness, and strengthen every person who may read it. If the book, or series, has been beneficial to you or someone you may know, please contact Hender-Tree Publications or visit *hendertree.com* to let us know. Your feedback is greatly appreciated.

Until the next time we explore another volume together in *The Leadership Series*, may Father GOD bless you, and may HE keep you in HIS arms.

Also Available

Heads of War...Volume 4
Belial...The Worthless One

ISBN : 978-1-9736-1281-0 (sc)
ISBN : 978-1-9736-1283-4 (hc)
ISBN : 978-1-9736-1282-7 (e)